MAKING DREAMS COME TRUE

WITHOUT MONEY, MIGHT OR MIRACLES

A Guide for Dream-Chasers and Dream-Catchers

Ivan H. Scheier

Anna M. Scidman
Contributing Editor

Library of Congress Cataloging-in-Publication Data

Scheier, Ivan H.
  Making dreams come true without money, might, or miracles : a guide for
  dream-chasers and dream-catchers/ Ivan H. Scheier ; contributing editor,
  Anna M. Seidman.
      p. cm.
  Includes bibliographical references.
  ISBN 0-940576-23-6 (pbk.)
  1. Voluntarism. I. Seidman, Anna. II. Title.

  HV49.V64 S34 2000
  361.3'7--dc21   00-049476

Copyright © 2000   Energize, Inc.
                          5450 Wissahickon Avenue
                          Philadelphia, PA 19144
                          www.energizeinc.com

ISBN 0-940576-23-6

 Printed on Recycled Paper

TABLE OF CONTENTS

Keep away from people who try to belittle your ambitions.
Small people always do that, but the really great make you feel that
you, too, can become great.
Mark Twain

FOREWORD

It was natural that Energize, Inc. would be committed to publishing this book. My dream was "caught" by Ivan over two decades ago and nothing has been the same since. My own experience attests to that fact that Ivan's role as Dream-Catcher has been a lifelong practice.

In 1974, Ivan was director of a Boulder-based organization then called the National Information Center on Volunteers in Courts and I was a novice director of volunteers for the Philadelphia Family Court. In those days we had a Pennsylvania state association specifically for justice volunteer programs and that group invited Ivan to fly in and be our trainer for a two-day conference. A week before the event, the association president called me in a dither to inquire whether I was free on Sunday night to pick Ivan up at the Philadelphia Airport, take him to dinner, and make sure he was settled at the hotel. I distinctly remember asking in amazement, "you mean all by myself?" Apparently no one else wanted to give up Sunday evening, while I saw this as an astonishing opportunity to spend time with someone so respected in our field.

Sunday arrived and so did Ivan. We had never met before and I found myself disarmed by this casual, friendly and unassuming man. Dinner lasted three hours and, as I remember it, Ivan kept asking *me* questions! Somehow, during the conversation we began to talk about the lack of written material in the field of volunteering. I mentioned, purely musing out loud, that I would love to write a history of volunteering in America—mainly to prove to skeptics how important volunteers have been since day one in this country, and to prove all the stereotypes about white, rich, old women wrong. Ivan nearly jumped out of his seat. "Do it!" he implored, "I'll be all the help I can." And that was the moment at which my random musing crystallized into a dream.

We spent more time talking about how important such a book could be and how hard the research might prove. The next morning, driving to the conference site, Ivan had more thoughts on the subject. The conference was wonderful and someone else took charge of hosting Ivan for the return trip. It was on the ride home from the conference with a colleague that I tossed out the following question: "How would you like to work with me on writing a history of volunteering in the United States?" Katie Noyes (today Campbell) cannot fully explain why, but she responded: "Might be fun."

Two days later I dropped Ivan a note to tell him that Katie and I had been discussing the project very seriously. He immediately responded that he would look into some funding possibilities. About a month later he mailed us a personal check for $50 (a significant sum in those days), attaching a note that urged us to move forward and expressing his hope that we would accept his contribution since he was not sure he could come up with outside funding at that time.

In 1978, Katie and I produced *By the People: A History of Americans as Volunteers*. It was the third book ever published specifically on the subject of volunteers. And it put me on a path that led to eight other books and the formation of Energize, Inc. Ivan not only caught my dream, he recognized it as a dream. We've remained supportive colleagues and good friends. Clearly, I had to produce this book for him, but the most important way I try to repay his mentorship in my life is to nurture the dreams of others. I have been a Dream-Catcher-in-Training at Ivan's knee for a long time. I hope that this book sparks dreaming, chasing and catching of all sorts. ◉

Susan J. Ellis
President, Energize, Inc.
Philadelphia, PA
August 2000

➤•◀)▸◉◀(▸•◀

Dedication

For every dreamer. . .

There are two ways of spreading light:
to be the candle or the mirror that reflects it.
Edith Wharton

INTRODUCTION

A world in which people have no chance of achieving their dreams is not, to me, a world in which I would choose to live. In support of this belief, I have written this book about dreams. The subject matter is not the reveries of sleep, but rather the imaginings, wishes, yearnings and aspirations that haunt both night and day. These are the visions and goals of central significance to the lives of both individuals and their communities.

Despite the great need for dreams, the vast majority of these visions die quickly, are stillborn, or are never even conceived. The emptiness that takes the place of dreams condemns millions to frustration, hopelessness, cynicism, bitterness and a loss of self-respect. An appalling societal deprivation results from all the dreams that have died and those that have never been born.

Of all the factors that inhibit or obstruct dreams, money, or the lack thereof, takes a starring role. Fortunately, the absence of funds need not doom a dream to failure. This book is about making dreams come true, especially when not much money is available. It will challenge the societal expectation that the realization of aspirations depends upon obtaining adequate funds to "purchase the dream." The truth is that there is rarely—or ever—enough money to do so. Many dreamers lose heart, or perhaps the stomach, to pursue their goals through the drastic compromises required by the search for funds. To avoid this trap, this book will concentrate on "budget dream-chasing"—finding creative ways to circumvent fundraising through volunteers, bartering and other innovative manipulation of available resources.

Some of the inspiration for this creative approach to dream-chasing came from my experiences with approximately 250 individuals who lived or visited VOLUNTAS: The Center for Creative Community, a retreat residence in Madrid, New Mexico between 1991-1996. VOLUNTAS provided attendees with a dream-friendly environment, aimed at stimulating creative, expansive and practical dreaming about volunteerism. Additional ideas came from my work with the 700 individuals who attended the 65 CHALLENGE Think Tanks/Reflection Pools that I facilitated throughout North America between 1985 and 1996.

Within these settings I met many "dreamers"—individuals with ideas, hopes and inspirations who lacked the financial resources to bring these dreams to life. In response, I took on the role of listener, encourager, facilitator, enabler and midwife to their dreams, a role I referred to as "Dream-Catcher." As self-appointed "Dream-Catcher" I have learned that I do not bear exclusive title to this calling. As I hope this book confirms, the role of "Dream-Catcher" could be your role too. Maybe it already is.

Finally and perhaps also initially is the admonition that the materials that follow are an overlapping set of readings. Although there is a certain logic to the sequential arrangement of these materials, you may nevertheless browse this book in any order that you wish. If you choose to read the material in a different order than presented, do not assume that by looking ahead you can learn how it all turns out.

We do not know that yet.

In considering death, Hamlet's concern was . . .

To sleep, perchance to dream,
Aye, there's the rub!

By contrast,
*To be **awake** and not to **dream** . . .*
is the condition that concerns us in this book.

CHAPTER 1

A Few Words . . . (well, maybe more than a few). . .

A more technical treatise than this one would probably commence with a section in which I, as author, would define the terms with which my readers might find themselves unfamiliar. In fact, in this first chapter, I offer my definitions and commentary on several of the terms (some of which I myself have coined) and the categories addressed in this book. My definitions are, however, anything but technical, and hopefully leave more than enough room for you, the reader, to contemplate and to find a way to insert my terminology into the context of your own experiences.

>-◄)►O‹(►-◄

Where there is no vision, the people perish.
Proverbs 29:18a

A Few Words about Dream-Catchers

Ojibwe (called the Chippewa) Native Americans believe that dreams, both good and bad, float through the air all day and night, searching for their destination. To help their children deal with dreams, the Ojibwe fashioned "dream catchers." A dream catcher is a device that resembles a spider web adorned with feathers. It is hung above a sleeping area in a location where it will catch the morning light. The dream catcher is designed to attract all sorts of dreams. Bad dreams that are attracted to the device do not know the way through and get caught in the webbing where the first light of day causes them to melt away and perish. Good dreams are more savvy than their nightmarish counterparts since they know the way through the hole in the center of the web and consequently are able to float down the feathers to the sleeper below. Traditionally, the dream catcher was adorned with owl feathers for wisdom and eagle feathers for courage.

The Dream-Catcher of this book shares some but not all characteristics with the Native American artifact. My Dream-Catcher is a person, not a device. He or she takes up the task of helping people achieve their dreams, where "dream" means a goal, a purpose, a cause or a vision (more in the purposive than the mystic sense). Like the Ojibwe device, the Dream-Catcher of this book will help filter these dreams. The human Dream-Catcher, however, filters out the harmful influences rather than the bad dreams. My Dream-Catcher acts like the webbing to impede the distractions and dissuasions that prevent an individual from realizing his or her pursuit. Similar to the Native American object, the Dream-Catcher will provide the feathers of wisdom and courage to enable the dreamer to focus on and to follow her or his true aspirations.

The individuals aided by the Dream-Catchers of this book are not sleepers, but instead are those with vision who seek the means to implement their ideas. These dreamers—or "Dream-Chasers"[1]—need encouragement, or perhaps simply the absence of *dis*couragement. On some occasions the Dream-Catcher can help the Dream-Chaser focus on that which is important or attainable, removing the distractions that inhibit and impede creative ideas. At times, the Dream-Catcher need only listen, giving the Dream-Chaser the forum to speak freely about goals and to find solutions around obstacles. In essence, the Dream-Catcher helps transform the Dream-Chaser into a Dream-Catcher, an individual capable of finding the way to achieve his or her goal.

I have spent a great deal of my professional life examining and encouraging visionary leadership of volunteer efforts. At first glance, this book may seem a departure from the types of management guidance I have offered in other writing. It isn't. Volunteering is uniquely intertwined with dreams. Why would anyone give time and talent, especially to address issues of the human condition, unless motivated by a vision that things could be better? Dream-Chasers need not always be volunteers, but often they cannot be bothered by such a small thing as the absence of money. There are things that matter as much as money, or more, in the world of dreams.

The core of my readership has always been people occupying the leadership roles of volunteer efforts. Whether called "directors of volunteers," "community resource mobilizers," or simply "presidents" of all-volunteer associations, such leaders have been urged by authors and trainers to focus on best management practices—and so they should. But perhaps it's time to return to some fundamental philosophies that can be overlooked in the organizing rush. Leaders of volunteers do not "direct" as much as they enable. They see the essence of a person and capture it, offering a channel for those talents to be useful to others. Often this process is not simply matching a

---

[1]My friend and colleague Eileen Cackowski helped me to coin the term "Dream-Chaser."

résumé to a job slot. Rather, enthusiasm, energy, and vision become the most important factors for volunteer success. This enabling often results in a serial effect. In helping volunteers achieve their dream of meaningful volunteering, coordinators of volunteers let loose upon the community, more and more Dream-Catchers.

Therefore, I hope my volunteerism colleagues will recognize their Dream-Catcher role and embrace it. The same applies to friends, colleagues, parents, teachers, and even the unsuspecting stranger who finds him or herself in the right place at the right time. Dream-Catchers can help Dream-Chasers realize their dreams—turning what might otherwise remain flights of fancy into wonderful reality. Maybe Dream-Catchers are as important to the process as are the dreamers.

Some years ago, this poem came to me as an expression of the powerful connection between being a volunteer and being a dreamer:

> *Once, volunteering was for dreamers . . .*
> *We were—and some still are—pioneers in*
> *compassionate enterprise. It was the way we*
> *got good things done before there were big budgets or*
> *bureaucracies.*
>
> *Once, volunteering was a legacy . . .*
> *It was inheritance from family, friends, or*
> *Faith, an unselfconscious way of living out*
> *basic values.*
> *Volunteering was just the way we were, a*
> *private matter of public consequence.*
>
> *Once, volunteering was a power . . .*
> *We didn't react to trends, we CAUSED them.*
> *We didn't supplement staff, we CREATED them.*
> *Politicians didn't use us; we used them.*
> *And we made dreams happen.*
>
> *Once, volunteering was for dreamers.*
> *May it soon be so again.*

><+>×O×<+><

Whatever you can do, or dream you can, begin it.
Boldness has genius, power and magic in it.
Johann Wolfgang von Goethe

A Few Words about Dreams

Although a Dream-Catcher can help facilitate any kind of dream, my role as Dream-Catcher has been to assist with goals that promise to enhance the quality of life in a community. These altruistic motivations are more often of the kind upon which one would focus deliberately during the day. However, these same aspirations also can, in mysterious ways, influence night dreams. Alternatively, nighttime reveries may trigger and otherwise inspire a person's ideas of how to help others.

Throughout my years as a self-appointed Dream-Catcher, many individuals have shared their aspirations, goals and hopes with me. Some of these dreams have a very concrete form while others are still evolving, and appear rather vague or general. Examples of these dreams include:

* To establish a national museum on the history of women;

* To educate and to assist people in the value and feasibility of alternative means of creating affordable housing (such as straw bale houses);

* To renovate old buildings, helping to revive a community;

* To rejuvenate an isolated Hispanic community whose young people currently have to leave in order to find work;

* To write an autobiography, illustrating what one person can do to change a rigid and suppressive system;

✳   To establish a performing dance facility;

✳   To channel a love and skill for producing films in a socially-positive direction that moves away from the current focus on sex and violence;

✳   To serve the birthing community by providing affordable health care to all women;

✳   To explore and help create situations of hope and healing, especially in regard to the dangers of nuclear waste;

✳   To help Bulgarians expand their understanding of (American-style) volunteerism;

✳   To create a community center in a village almost totally without financial or other resources;

✳   To create a village-based healing practice and an infirmary "health hostel" using donated resources;

✳   To create a market in America for the work of Romanian artists (so that the artists do not feel that they need to emigrate and thus deprive their own country of their talent).

✳   Your dream here:_____

Not every dreamer who confided in me aspired to change the world or to rescue some segment of the world's population. Many of the dreams that others disclosed seemed small by comparison to the ones that set out to create communities, museums, programs and markets. Often individuals revealed the simple desire to improve life for no one other than themselves. For example, I recall one individual who simply aspired to find a way to live closer to his own personal values.

I have learned over time not to underestimate the potential value and impact of these "small" and sometimes "self-oriented" dreams. Every fulfilled dream has the potential for triggering more dreams and for freeing others to pursue their dreams. Take, for example, the individual who sought to free herself of the need for money (insofar as that was possible) in order to devote greater time to community service. Despite its less than monumental focus, this individual's dream had a vast potential for a ripple effect. An individual who devotes greater time to community service may free those served to chase their own dreams. Thus every dream, no matter how small or how self-oriented, may ultimately enable the monumental dreams of others.

True dreams, by their nature, are to some extent selfishly motivated. Even individuals with truly altruistic goals should receive some personal benefit from the actualization of their aspirations. In my opinion, all helping should be "happy helping." In other words, whenever possible, reaching out to others should not have to hurt before it helps. One of the reasons that I started the VOLUNTAS residence in the first place was as a response to what I viewed as the martyr-strewn volunteer landscape, a situation I considered deplorable and unnecessary. Too many individuals had lost themselves in the effort to aid others. Perhaps they had become injured in the process of following the "wrong dream," wrong for them because these individuals had forgotten that they themselves were to be among the dream's beneficiaries.

Any dream, whether primarily altruistic or basically self-serving, can be the "right dream." There is in fact no such thing as a "bad dream," with the exclusive exceptions of dreams that are knowingly immoral or illegal, such as those that would require trampling other equally or more qualified people who seek the same goal. The extreme example might be the dream to become the top or sole drug dealer in a territory centering on a local Junior High School.

In stark contrast to the foregoing example are at least three appropriate types of self-oriented dreams, all of which can benefit by the suggestions offered within this book. They include:

1) *Dreams that involve clearing the ground for later, more other-oriented helping in the wider community.* Examples of this would include individuals who envision easing social obligations, consistent with ethics, in order to find the time and financial ability to focus on others. A man who dreams of retiring after working for 45 years may use his newly found free time to offer volunteer mentor services to young professionals. A woman who dreams of finding inexpensive adult day care for her elderly mother might use the time she gains to spend a few hours each day with her grandchildren, freeing her daughter to pursue her own career.

Some with self-oriented aspirations recognize the potential altruistic benefits only after they have achieved their initial goals. For example, a woman aspired to be a part of diplomatic society, hoping that her husband, a career State Department official, would be appointed the U.S. Ambassador to Croatia. Although she longed for the personal benefits connected to her role as wife of the Ambassador (the excitement, the travel, etc.) she soon learned that her position afforded her a great deal of power and access to help others. Two years into her husband's posting, she has organized and orchestrated numerous projects to help orphans, land mine victims and other members of the Croatian community.

2) *Dreams that serve the dreamer at the same time that they serve others.* This sharing of benefits articulates the "people approach;" an attempt to ensure that, insofar as possible, people get satisfaction for themselves at the same time that they help others.[2]

Even the simplest act of helping someone else generally tends to be a very self-satisfying experience. Any mother who has patiently taught her little one to tie his shoes, can tell you about the pleasure she experiences at the triumphant smile of the child who finally accomplishes the task on his own.

---

[2]For a more detailed discussion of this subject, refer to my book, *Building Staff/Volunteer Relations,* Philadelphia: Energize, Inc., 1993.

My personal example is VOLUNTAS. In creating the residence, I truly believed that a significant number of other people, especially people wounded in the community activism war, could use the relative peace and quiet there. I soon learned that *so could I.* The same is true for my current dream project, Stillpoint.

3) *Dreams that neither accompany nor clearly lead to helping others.* In this category are dreams of a truly personal nature. Believe it or not, examples for this category do not come easily, since most self-oriented dreams result in benefits to others. Take for example, the writer who wishes to publish a best-seller. Her ostensibly selfish effort may win her the fame and fortune she seeks, but it could not occur unless millions of people find enjoyment and entertainment between the covers of her book. An individual who dreams of winning the lottery might likely use the money to make more charitable donations (even if only for the tax benefits) or might at least stop being a financial burden or worry to some loved one.

True examples of purely self-oriented dreaming might involve someone who has the desire to get an advanced degree in an esoteric subject, say Sanskrit Literature, entirely for personal edification, without even the desire to teach it to others. Alternatively, another dreamer might aspire to write significant poetry without caring whether anyone else ever reads or understands it. In both cases, and others like these, self-oriented dreamers have a perfect, ethical right to their dreams. Indeed, if we are on this planet in hopes of making it a happier, more fulfilling place, we should remember that each happy, fulfilled individual member contributes to the emotional health of the whole community.

>+<>:O+<>+<

To fulfill a dream, to be allowed to sweat over lonely labor, to be given the chance to create, is the meat and potatoes of life. The money is the gravy. As everyone else, I love to dunk my crust in it. But alone, it is not a diet designed to keep body and soul together.
Bette Davis

A Few Words about Money

My insights about money have been rare enough so that I can remember both of them. One, remembered shortly after recovery from Economics 101 in college, was that money is not mainly about numbers, statistics, graphs and somewhat scientific laws. Money is largely about feelings. I said I "remembered" this because it was not the first time I had encountered this concept. I first became cognizant of the juxtaposition of money and feelings when I came to my first financial awareness during the Great Depression. I should never have forgotten it. In retrospect, I now note with interest that the very word "Depression" refers to feelings as well as economic conditions.

People often have pretty strong feelings about making money, spending money, and losing money. Money can even be blamed for many of the relational problems shared by couples. Lack of money certainly stirs strong feelings in most people. Therefore, I might have stirred emotional flutterings had I simply entitled this book: "Making Dreams Come True *Without Much Money*." Would such a title have suggested a peculiar exclusion of the preferable way to get things done, wherever possible? Not necessarily!

Yes indeed, we must have enough money, or its equivalent in resources, for the basics of food, shelter and clothing. In fact, I see desirable commodities falling into three distinct categories. In the first category are the lovely things that money cannot buy, like love, friendship, and peace of mind. (Indeed, research conducted by the

New Road Map Foundation[3] suggests clearly that, *above a survival level there is no overall correlation between income level and self-rated happiness/fulfillment.*)

In the second category are the things that only money can buy such as a nice house or car.

It is the third category that this book focuses upon: *Things money can buy that might also be obtained without money* (if you don't have it and can't get it). In short, this book is about creativity, ingenuity and finding non-monetary solutions to pursuing dreams of almost any kind.

Consider the following analogy. Within a certain range of distance, often seeming to begin as little as 100 feet, Americans typically get from point A to point B by car. So much so that if you ask how far it is from one place to another you will often get the driving time, not the miles. (For some there are actually two driving times; one for low traffic and a second for high traffic trips.) But what does someone do without a car, or if it breaks down and there are none available to either rent or borrow? The philosophy of this book applied to that situation would be: Don't give up! Instead find another way to get from point A to point B, such as using public transportation, riding a bicycle, or simply walking (although the third alternative would be contraindicated for a trip from Los Angeles to San Diego). The selection of one of these alternatives can lead to unexpected benefits. For example, a bicyclist or pedestrian might see and enjoy more of the surroundings and would undoubtedly get some good exercise. (And to think that I used to have friends who *drove* three blocks to their health club!)

This book encourages those who chase dreams to apply the same creative approach. If you cannot raise the money to help achieve your dream, look at non-financially oriented alternatives. In fact, this book will concentrate on those other ways, since I believe such alternatives tend to be neglected in our society's predisposition to think dollars first. In looking at the bicycle paths, so to speak, this book does not deny the reality or necessity of superhighways in contem-

---

[3]New Road Map Foundation, P.O. Box 15981, Seattle WA 98115, (206) 527-0437.

porary society. Nonetheless, the idea of exploring ways in which dreams can be achieved "without much money" does not imply disregard for money. It simply recognizes that there is not nearly enough money to make all worthy dreams come true. By the same token, there are some dreams for which no amount of money would ever be enough.

And yet . . . money definitely does help to achieve a multitude of worthy goals, and is virtually the only way to achieve some goals.

So why, throughout this book, do I neglect or exclude the dream of the very pursuit of wealth itself? Frankly, this is a position harder to defend.

I recognize and respect a person's right to use money earned, for creature comforts as well as necessities. (This would include necessities such as this book, for example!) I certainly recognize and respect the intention to earn money for philanthropic purposes. Nevertheless, this book does not deal with "making (lots of) money" as a dream. The main reason is that others have already dealt with it, frequently and far better than I could! I must also admit the sheer inadequacy of any advice I might offer. I have never succeeded in making much money, and basically have never even really tried. So, for me to propose my thoughts on the subject could prove worse than the blind leading the blind. It could amount to the blind leading the *sighted*!

Beyond that, I would not, of course, want to deal with dreams in which the money might either be acquired or used unethically. In cases where the goals are worthy, or seem so, why not deal directly with the goals themselves instead of focusing on but one means of achieving them: money. Take, for example, an individual who would like to build a women's shelter. This Dream-Chaser has a greater chance of bringing her dream to fruition by focusing upon the shelter itself rather than upon the money it would take to finance the dream. Perhaps an articulate campaign would persuade someone to donate a building, or perhaps local authorities could channel the community service efforts of recovering spousal abusers into construction work. A Dream-Chaser who thinks creatively can dodge financial obstacles.

Most Dream-Chasers with whom I have had the pleasure to interact share a single attribute—they do not have nearly enough money to purchase their dreams outright. With each of them, I consistently and decisively offered the following advice:

Do not sit down and write a big grant, and
Do not sit down and write a small grant, either.

A Dream-Chaser is not a grant writer. The fuller job description is:

Making Dreams Happen—Without Much Money

This is where dream-chasing connects to volunteerism in the broadest sense. Dream-Chasers find ways to involve community volunteers widely, deeply and trustfully and learn how to creatively scrounge other community resources.

The same philosophy can apply to any type of dream, even those that are of a more personal, self-oriented nature, such as getting a college education. Acquiring the requisite amount of money to defray all costs is but one way of achieving the goal. A more creative approach would include seeking out special programs offered by employers, community agencies, and even the educational institution itself. The key is to look beyond the price tag to the goal itself— the college degree.

Creativity, ingenuity, and inventiveness may all be far more valuable gifts than money. Sadly, I frequently hear people tell me that they "are not creative." Strangely, these same people are often the ones who have dreams to reach out to their communities. Anyone who can dream can be creative and thus anyone who can dream can find ways to fulfill their aspirations "without much money."

Epilogue: If anyone still believes I hate money, I invite you to call my bluff and send me some.

>+‹›·O‹‹›+‹

*The reasonable man adapts himself to the world; the unreasonable one
persists in trying to adapt the world to himself.
Therefore all progress depends on the unreasonable man.*
George Bernard Shaw

A Few Words about Barriers and Bigots

This book is about barriers to human aspiration and how to
remove them. The book deals with one important kind of blockage,
the kind that an individual can deal with, as an individual, in pursuit
of a dream, goal or vision. Examples of such potentially surmount-
able barriers include access to relevant information, minimizing of
environmental distractions, and development of an effective support
system. A key figure in this support system is the Dream-Catcher,
and most of this book defines the role of that person.

There is a second kind of barrier which this book generally does
not deal with, the kind that individuals are ordinarily unable to overcome on their own. These "social barriers" are deeply embedded in
law, regulation, bigoted custom and perception. They are why a
woman who dreams of becoming a CEO is likely to have a harder
time achieving that goal than a man with the same level of skill and
talent. They are why an African-American who is interested in a
white-dominated social club, often has less chance of being invited;
why a disabled person may lack access to a place of business fully
open to other people; why a low-income person is often assumed to
be "lazy" and not worth taking a chance on as an employee—even
before being *given* a chance.

Any society that considers itself a free society, or on the way to
becoming one, must confront such barriers as a society, via education, changes in law and regulation and, if necessary, non-violent
social protest actions as, for example, in the women's suffrage and
civil rights movements.

In fact, a society committed to full opportunity for all its members, must actively seek to minimize and remove *both* kinds of barriers, those that can be challenged as an individual and those that must be tackled by society as a whole. This book happens to concentrate on "individual" barriers because that is what I know most about. Moreover, the two can be related. Within the range of growth still permitted by social barriers, there almost always remains a difference between those who are willing to try to reach their goals and, in spite of frustration, do so to their utmost, and those who are not willing to try, and who may actually blame social barriers as a reason for not trying. For example, in spite of discrimination against women in the workplace, an increasing number of talented, committed and courageous women have succeeded in becoming CEOs. In so doing, I believe they are raising and someday will utterly shatter the very glass ceiling that unjustly hampered their career efforts in the first place.

The principle is, I believe: If enough people in a discriminated-against class go on to achieve anyhow, in spite of social barriers and raw bigotry, they will ultimately help remove those barriers. That *doesn't* in any way excuse current injustices; it simply suggests another way in which social barriers can be eliminated—along with education, legislation and social advocacy, not as a substitute for them. And always, there is the fulfillment associated with achievement for the individual, as an individual, within whatever range social barriers allow, regardless of impact on social barriers.

As a kind of personal footnote, my passion for helping people make their dreams come true was ignited in the first place by my experiences with social barriers—how they suppressed and dehumanized people, and how their removal freed people up to reach the fullest expression of their humanity. The last chapter recounts some of that....

>·<>·O·<>·<

*Yes, I am a dreamer. For a dreamer is one who can find his way
by moonlight, and see the dawn before the rest of the world.*
Oscar Wilde

A Few Words about Organizations

As you read through this book, you will notice a rather glaring omission. Almost without exception I refer to individuals as dreamers and ignore organizations. It is not that I believe that organizations are incapable of dreaming. I even believe that the principles developed herein for individual Dream-Chasers can be applied to organizations, at least analogously.

So why the omission? First of all, it is because I do not know enough about organizations to write intelligently about their characteristics. I defer that role to someone with the appropriate expertise.

Still the potential for the Dream-Chaser's interaction with an organization is too significant to ignore. The probability of such an event does not render it easy or even desirable in all cases. One of the tasks a Dream-Catcher will assume in the effort to assist a potential Dream-Chaser will be to decide when and whether to affiliate with a like-minded organization. It would be so simple if a Dream-Catcher could say to the dreamer: "Look, just be clear about your vision, find an organization that shares it and join up." Occasionally this is the appropriate advice. More often than not the price of affiliation is too dear and the process of collaborating much less straight-forward than it may seem at first glance.

Complications arise from difficulties in finding the right organization. Often the perfect organization is simply not accessible to the individual Dream-Chaser. For those organizations that are both visible and accessible there lies another issue in the contradictions between an organization's *professed* goal or dream and what it actually does.

Organizations themselves are often motivated in part if not greatly by the need to preserve themselves. Part of this motivation is also served by the preservation of the status quo. These characteristics run afoul of the creativity that Dream-Chasers need to realize their vision. That is not to say that organizations are entirely bereft of this ingenuity. In fact, in the history of an organization that is genuinely devoted to a dream, there is often some incandescent individual or small group of individuals. However, sadly, much of the inventiveness is often lost in the organization's effort to maintain itself.

This book does not intend to discourage the potential interaction of dreamers with organizations. It does, however, emphasize the kind of creative, innovative dream that is far enough ahead of its time so that it is more likely to *found* an organization than to *find* one. And as these new organizations develop, their founding Dream-Chasers should not forget their own origins and in doing so should make an effort to learn much more about ways in which individuals and organizations can interface in the pursuit of dreams.

><+><O><>+<

The great thing in this world is not so much where we stand,
as in what direction we are moving.
Oliver Wendell Holmes

A Few Words About...Ivan

Ivan Scheier authored almost every word that you will read in this book about Dream-Catching. This brief section about Ivan is a bit of a departure from the rest of the text. When I was asked to assume the role of contributing editor of this book, I encountered an inspired manuscript, full of honesty, creativity and insight—the type of material that is unmistakably Ivan's.

I did, however, notice one serious omission—a biography of Ivan himself—without which many of the comments, suggestions and

musings could potentially lose the context that enhance their meaning. Therefore I recommended the addition of a narrative about Ivan
in order to reveal the circumstances that contributed to his becoming
a Dream-Catcher. Not surprisingly, I was called upon to write this
narrative. I had but one disability to overcome—the fact that though
I had read much of his written material, I had never met or spoken to
Ivan. As we lived hundreds of miles apart, and as my schedule and
budget left no margin for a face-to-face meeting, I conducted an inter-
view by telephone.

Within the first five minutes I was disarmed by a man whose
eclectic array of experiences had endowed him with the motivation
not only to chase his own dreams but to seek ways to help others to
do the same. More than that I was charmed by his endearing ability
to laugh at himself. The following is but a distillation of the story he
shared with me.

Anna Seidman, Contributing Editor

Ivan Scheier—Dream-Catcher of VOLUNTAS

A brief description of Ivan Scheier's life shows the inevitable path
that led him to write this book. Although he did not invent dream-
catching, he coined the phrase from his experiences leading up to
and during his self-appointed role of "Dream-Catcher in Residence"
of VOLUNTAS, a retreat residence that operated between 1990 and
1996 in Madrid, New Mexico.

Ivan's background started him far from VOLUNTAS and dream-
catching both physically and philosophically. He grew up in
Plattsburgh, New York, a small town in the upper part of the state.
He literally skipped through school and found himself a freshman at
Union College on scholarship at the age of 16. After two years, he left
college to serve with the military in World War II. He returned to
Union to complete his major in philosophy and minors in psycholo-
gy and French. During graduate work in philosophy at Harvard
University, he became convinced that he was not a professional
philosopher and transferred to McGill University in Montreal,

Canada where ultimately he obtained his master's and doctorate in psychology.

In the years that followed, Ivan moved around a bit, teaching psychology at different colleges and universities and later working for several years as a junior research scientist in statistical psychology at the University of Illinois. He came to find his life choices unfulfilling, realizing that his dreams lay elsewhere. In 1960, he decided to take a sabbatical from his research duties and moved to Boulder, Colorado in order to write a book. He never did write the book, but he did fall in love with Boulder and his sabbatical extended to a stay of 23 years.

The assassination of John F. Kennedy upended Ivan's existence. Like many Americans, Ivan was shocked by the abrupt and meaningless tragedy of Kennedy's death. Unlike others, Ivan sought to find some meaning from the circumstances that led to the assassination. He looked retrospectively at his own achievements and recognized a need to change direction and to find a way to reach out to others to try to prevent similar horrific incidents. He took it upon himself to study Kennedy's killer, learning that Lee Harvey Oswald had been a troubled child who had been brought to the attention of the juvenile justice system. His research showed that the judicial authorities who recognized Oswald's problems lacked the time to intervene and simply booted Oswald back into society. Ivan believed that, had Oswald's early encounter with the juvenile system turned out differently, it could have prevented the Kennedy murder. Ivan decided that he could use his knowledge of psychology to help the overburdened juvenile justice system and to hopefully prevent others like Oswald from falling through the cracks.

Recognizing the budget constraints of the justice system, Ivan decided to offer his services on a volunteer basis. He contacted Bud Holmes, a friend who was one of the few juvenile judges in the country who allowed volunteers to serve in his courtrooms. Ivan ultimately served for ten years as a court psychologist in the Boulder County juvenile probation department on both paid and volunteer status. Later, he became coordinator of volunteers in one of the few counties in the country that employed an organized volunteer program in their juvenile court system.

The success of the volunteer effort became hard to ignore and eventually, Ivan decided to share it with others in need. He wrote about their progress, started consulting and offering seminars. In the late 1960's he and others involved in the volunteer effort formed a distinct nonprofit organization called The National Information Center on Volunteers in Courts. Soon it became obvious that the problems faced by children needed more help than could be offered exclusively by the legal system. Volunteers in all forms of human services joined in the effort and ultimately the organization, headed by Ivan, changed its name to The National Information Center on Volunteerism.

The success of this organization led to another pivotal point in Ivan's path toward dream-catching. A merger with a similarly sized organization, in the supposed interest of unity and efficiency, turned out, in Ivan's opinion, to be more of a takeover by that organization. Also about that time, an attempt to form a national coalition of voluntary organizations, which he helped to instigate and direct, seemed to him more prone to squabble and wobble than trust and thrust ahead. Talk about dreams turning sour!!! Disgruntled and disenchanted with large volunteer organizations, Ivan moved on to free-lance, write, consult, and offer seminars.

The consulting life led Ivan to take another close look at his accomplishments and dreams. He had created a smooth presentation of ostensibly valuable information, yet he had no first hand knowledge of the practicality of the advice he offered. He realized that he offered seminar after seminar yet never witnessed his recommendations in practice. He became concerned that his polished presentation might lack substance. He decided he needed to stay long enough with a community to witness their efforts based upon his teachings. This realization led to the third pivotal movement in Ivan's route toward dream-catching. For three years, he volunteered (for travel and expense reimbursement only) around the United States and Canada, at a total of 47 locations.

Witnessing the efforts of the grass-roots volunteer movement proved a sobering experience. In the attempt to provide community leadership and service, people were being trampled emotionally. People were tired, frustrated and overworked. Ivan saw a great need for healing. He settled in New Mexico and developed a small organization called the Center for Creative Community, offering mini-retreats for two to three people at a time at his small house in Santa Fe to help them refocus and rejuvenate their volunteer spirit. He became frustrated at the limits of his ability to reach out to the many in need. His dream to create a larger scale retreat instigated VOLUNTAS.

At VOLUNTAS, which is described in more detail in another chapter, Ivan created a larger scale retreat/residence where people could come to heal, rejuvenate and dream. Ivan became the "Dream-Catcher-in-residence" and learned from personal experience the tools and pitfalls of full-time dream-catching.

When VOLUNTAS closed in 1996, Ivan moved to Stillpoint, a self-help retreat center in Truth or Consequences, New Mexico, a complex of nine buildings housed on seven adjoining lots. To date, approximately 200 people have visited Stillpoint, most of whom have contributed to its development and upkeep. Some have stayed a few days, while others have stayed as long as seven or eight months. Ivan no longer refers to himself as "Dream-Catcher." At Stillpoint, he prefers to be recognized as "host." He is less invasive in the lives and the musings of the residents. He believes in allowing people to heal themselves and gives participants the space and the encouragement they need to do so.

Ivan's dreams of VOLUNTAS, Stillpoint and dream-catching were the result of three seminal events that propelled him toward his current direction. The Kennedy assassination pointed him in the direction of volunteering and helping others. The demise of the volunteer organization he had founded moved him away from large, organized service towards individual action. His effort to act on his own advice showed him the magnitude of "dreamicide," and the need for a place where dreams and dreamers can be healed, nurtured and facilitated.

Ivan's knowledge of dream-catching results in part from his formal training in psychology but also from his informal educational experiences, including his training in dance, holistic healing, Reiki, tai chi, and meditation. Perhaps more than anything, he has learned from the dreamers with whom he has had contact through the years.

At age 75, residing at Stillpoint, Ivan is living his "dream come true" and he is still dreaming. ◉

Rose-colored glasses are never made in bifocals.
Nobody wants to read the small print in dreams.
Ann Landers

CHAPTER TWO

The Rules of the Game

Now that we've defined the terms and introduced some of the philosophies that are central to dream-catching and dream-chasing, it is time to move on to the preliminary instructions. Perhaps the most important rule for both dreamers and Dream-Catchers is that "No Rule Is Absolute." As you read through the suggestions and recommendations offered within the ensuing pages, you will be struck by the seemingly myriad contradictions. In one section, for example, the Dream-Catchers will learn to avoid organizations, yet another will suggest that the Dream-Catcher find a like-minded organization for the dreamer to join. One portion of the book first tells dreamers to seek out as much information as they can and then later in the same section, dreamers are told that they may have to ignore the available information. These seeming inconsistencies speak to the nuances of dream-catching and dream-chasing. No one set of rules or techniques can apply to every dream or to every dreamer. A method that fails for one individual will offer the perfect solution for another. To understand the nuances, readers should concentrate as much on the explanations behind the recommendations as upon the recommendations themselves.

Don't Just Do Something. Sit There!
Sign from the Harriet Naylor Library
VOLUNTAS, Madrid, New Mexico 1990-1996

Rules for Dream-Catchers

Dream-Catchers fit no single job description. They fill many roles in society and come from a multitude of backgrounds. A few pursue dream-catching (though rarely under that name) as a major part of their worklife. Others perform it quite unconsciously, simply as part of their way of interacting with others. This book hopes to make the Dream-Catcher lifestyle both more conscious and effective, but this is an important thing people can do more of right now as a part-time rather than a full-time "job description." Whatever your job, you can be a Dream-Catcher along with it, and outside work hours, too. Anytime, anywhere. That said, helpful dream-catching techniques vary as do the settings in which such assistance is provided.

Despite their differences, most Dream-Catchers do share some essential characteristics. The following list of rules offers my suggestions of the fundamental elements for successful dream-catching. Although they appear as a list, the individual rules overlap and interact. Though I refer to them as rules, they are not to be rigidly enforced. A Dream-Catcher must learn, as I have, how and when to apply each of these principles to best aid the individual Dream-Chaser:

✱ *Allow dreamers to find their own way of dreaming.* Dream-Catchers must be careful to resist the temptation to tell people what to do, rather than to allow them to discover it for themselves. Nowhere is this structuring tendency more ridiculous than trying to tell people "how to reflect" in their quiet time. Nonetheless, one can still remind Dream-Chasers of the virtues of indirection, of not hitting things head-on all the time, of actually "looking the other way" sometimes. The Dream-Catcher should generally discourage the dreamer from assuming that the dream can be found or finalized on a deliberate, scheduled basis.

Instead, it should be more like deliberately trying to remember a name. The harder you try, the more elusive the memory becomes. Once you have stopped trying to pressure it, the name can at any time pop "spontaneously" into your mind (usually at 3:00 in the morning). Similarly, to see something better at twilight, they say you should first look a little away from it. In other words, the dreamer should not feel guilty about going to a movie, for instance listening to music, going shopping, or taking a nap. In their way, each of these activities can actually be part of the incubation process.

✱ *Learn when to leave people alone.* A Dream-Catcher must be able to resist the itch to intervene. More positively, s/he must be armed with the willingness—and the skill—to give people personal space, psychologically as well as physically. At times, this will stretch the Dream-Catcher's tolerance of ambiguity as well as the personal need to organize other people. Beyond the "hands-off" talent, this can involve a kind of deliberate engineering of the environment to encourage peacefulness and at the same time to provide a safe environment for passion—two rather different conditions. This apparent interaction of contradictions brings to mind the strange old blessing: "May God deny you peace, and grant you glory" (Miguel de Unamuno).

✱ *Listen when people want to talk.* When Dream-Chasers are allowed uninterrupted time to talk things through for themselves, they are far more likely to arrive at clear and meaningful conclusions than when someone is talking *at* them. (An incredible proportion of the Dream-Chasers with whom I have spent my time—including quite a few executive types—remarked on how rare and wonderful an experience it was to be really listened to, especially over an extended period, with concentration. While this was satisfying feedback for me as a Dream-Catcher, it was also a pretty horrifying comment on the communication practices of contemporary society as a whole.)

Part of being a good listener is knowing when *not* to talk. A Dream-Catcher needs to resist the urge to fill white spaces in people's thinking with his or her own goals and methods. Good intentions be damned! By injecting personal opinions, the Dream-Catcher may inadvertently subvert the Dream-Chaser's ownership of the dream. (Once, while assisting a woman who was casting about for an occupation with greater altruistic components, I advocated a new career of my own devising. I pushed my idea so hard and in such detail, that she has never consulted me again. Can you blame her?)

Instead of superimposing their own goals onto the Dream-Chaser's ideas, successful Dream-Catchers should emulate the effective community organizer, who carefully identifies the goals of those with whom s/he is working and then helps them achieve those goals.

* *Speak wisely when invited.* Once the Dream-Catcher perceives that the dreamer has developed a concrete goal of her or his own design, only then does the time for talking commence. Not unexpectedly the Dream-Catcher's words must be selected wisely. There are three main ingredients to the Dream-Catcher's input. These are *Affirmation, Information,* and *Connections.*

Affirmation. Dream-Catchers should offer a positive atmosphere to encourage the fulfillment of dreams. They should communicate the sense that achievement is at least conceivable in the light of resolute optimism. Nonetheless, affirmation does not equate to the endorsement of every dream. For example, a Dream-Catcher should not feel compelled to encourage a goal that is ethically unacceptable.

Affirmation means the willingness to deviate from the kind of conventional wisdom that must analyze dreams through "critical thinking." Such wisdom frequently ends up concentrating on finding flaws with a plan and thus shooting holes in the hopes of those with unconventional ideas. Why not encourage by offering ten reasons why something *could* be done rather than ten reasons why it should fail? A healthy compromise between resolute optimism and critical thinking would provide both lists.

An alternative approach to affirmation involves choosing words to make things sound better than they are. Countries that used to spy on each other, now gather "intelligence." People rarely die anymore; they "pass away" or "transition." Toilets are "rest rooms." Of course, as with anything else, one can take this approach too far. I once wrote an entire book in which people never had "problems," they only had "opportunities for improvement." Come on! Tact is fine and insults are not. But even in its early stages, pervasive euphemism obscures clarity in communication. So, if you cannot call it like it is, at least don't call it something else. Let your affirmations take the form of genuine encouragement and not mere word games.

Information. Part of the role of Dream-Catcher is to act as a conduit for information. A Dream-Catcher should provide information, on demand, in as many accessible channels as possible, including:

- personal experience
- computer networks
- a good library
- a network of informed people (in person or via the telephone, e-mail, etc.)

Information is the safety net that makes dream-chasing more than mere escapism. However, the bearer of information carries a heavy burden. Access to information tends to inject more realism into dreams.

Connections. Connections and information are inextricably inter-twined with connections serving as one of the greatest pipelines to information. A Dream-Catcher should have the humility and sensitivity to recognize that s/he is not the expert on all things. In many cases, a Dream-Catcher's most valuable role will come from enabling the Dream-Chaser to talk to some other especially relevant person. One of the Dream-Catcher's duties in this endeavor will be to thoroughly investigate the qualifications and expertise of those whom s/he intends to use as references. One who provides a connection of untested value merely "cops out" of the role of Dream-Catcher.

* *Let people define their own roles in their own dreams.* When people are ready to involve themselves in the work at hand, the Dream-Catcher must be prepared to permit and to encourage these Dream-Chasers to define what that work will be and how they will deal with it. Dream-Catchers must be able to cultivate a type of "adult Montessori" atmosphere.

* *Function as a "blinder finder."* A true Dream-Catcher must be pervasively paranoid about rigid preconceptions that restrict realistic consideration of alternatives. "Blinders" may exist with-in the dreamer's own mind, stemming from years of conditioning by conventional society. Dream-Chasers who do not carry their own blinders are often waylaid by nay-saying family members, friends, co-workers or individuals in authority. The Dream-Catcher must help to buffer the dreamer from the advice of those who would apply conventional wisdom to poke holes in the dream. (The potentially detrimental effects of conventional wis-dom are addressed in greater detail in chapter 4.) A few examples of potential blinders include:

  • *"The only (or main) way to achieve your dream is to calculate its purchase price and then go get the money."* This blinder is based upon the potentially erroneous assumption that every dream must arrive bearing a price tag.

- *"If you don't succeed in fulfilling your entire dream, you have failed."* This blinder is based upon the "all-or-none" fallacy. It assumes that partial realization of a dream represents failure, rather than, quite possibly, a way-station on the road to success.
- *"The only way to change a system is by trying to get people who have power in the system to do what you want them to do."* This blinder assumes that one must travel traditional pathways, e.g., lobbying government officials, petitioning the school board, etc. in order to stimulate change. Sometimes this assumption unrealistically precludes the option of creating your own alternative system, even a relatively small one—*to start.*

Instead of trying to impact the local school board, why not build a home-schooling network with the future dream of someday becoming an alternative school? (Note how this approach dovetails with the idea, discussed just above, of accepting partial accomplishments as stepping stones toward fulfilling a more extensive dream.) Instead of trying to persuade hostile or unenthusiastic government officials to protect public lands for public use, raise private funds to secure such lands. Such is the insight underlying the Nature Conservancy.

✱ *Serve as a practical prophet.* Dream-Catchers are futurists; that is, they can take a Dream-Chaser's action plan and run it out in at least several alternative future scenarios, creatively and plausibly. Although practicality is essential, it is the creative component that recognizes that dream-catching is not Newtonian physics. Where human yearning is involved, trends bend, bounce, and blend in ways more artistic than scientific. Indeed, two of the best Dream-Catchers I have ever met were artists before they became experts on voluntary action.[1]

---

[1] For more about practical prophesy, see my article, "Images of the Future," *The Journal of Volunteer Administration*, Vol. XIV, No. 1, Fall, 1995.

✳ *Be patient and persistent at the same time.* Most dreams take time, so the Dream-Catcher should be prepared to remain in contact with the Dream-Chaser and to continue to function as Dream-Catcher even after the dreamer has moved back or on to other activities. Your "stay in touch" efforts should be far more than perfunctory. Indeed, the dream-chase often has no definable ending. So, if they do not call or write, maybe *you* should . . . .

✳ *Be comfortable with being peculiar.* Dream-Catchers rarely conform to society's expectations. In fact, their very existence tends to make society uncomfortable. They spend much of their time focusing on someone other than themselves. They encourage people to dream and to do what society often says is impossible. A Dream-Catcher's list of peculiarities includes:

> *Restraint.* In our aggressive "go out and do it" society, Dream-Catchers often employ the strength to *avoid* doing something over the temptation to do something.

> *Flexibility.* Unlike many job descriptions, Dream-Catchers can flick in and out of their role, even during office hours.

> *Self-help.* A person may serve as his or her own Dream-Catcher just by being quiet, listening to him or herself and dodging blinders.

The last may be the greatest peculiarity of all. For we are all Dream-Catchers.
Because we are all dreamers.

⊁⊰⊁⊙⊀⊁⊰

Nothing happens unless first a dream.
Carl Sandburg

Rules for Dreamers

As indicated earlier, all dreams are beneficial, whether they benefit only the dreamer or society as a whole, so long as they are neither illegal nor immoral. The suggestions below apply as well to someone whose goal is to pay off the mortgage as to someone who wishes to promote world peace.

* *Do not be discouraged when nothing happens.* Nothing much happens anyhow, at first, so stay with it. Good things hardly ever hurry and inertia erodes hope. Do not let it. Be patient through the uneventful periods by living close to your beliefs every day.

* *Be wary of but not totally closed to change and compromise.* The only constants are the values that underlie the vision. Nothing happens exactly as first visualized. Do not expect it to. Reality is too complicated and surprise can be half the fun.
    Although it is wise to be flexible, try to keep compromise to a minimum, even when compromise is called nice names like "team-building," "negotiation" or "consensus." None of these concepts were invented to aid imagination. On the other hand, keep listening. Even though "creative" rarely wins an argument with "safe," the discussion that ensues may give rise to inventive ideas from surprising sources.

* *Do not be afraid to share your dream and the credit.* Seek out and encourage cooperators. Look for overlap in yearning and purpose. Dreams rarely survive their solo origins without evolution

to broader ownership. Get your ideas out there in the universe and watch to see who else is willing to fly.

If others choose to work with you, fine. If not, just hope they "do it right." Be reasonably sure that others will do it differently. Do not spend too much time hoping that you will get sufficient credit. People who crave credit tend to stick with safe and easy endeavors. Dreams rarely bear these characteristics. So get comfortable with vicarious victories and secret satisfactions. Of utmost importance is that the dream will happen somehow, somewhere at sometime and by somebody. Do not waste time fantasizing that you alone will make it happen and get the glory. You can hope that the one who gets the glory will be someone you can like and respect. But do not count on that either.

Dream-sharing often goes in both directions. Chances are you "stole" your idea from someone else, and it is unlikely that you even remember when or from whom. If it is really a good idea, various versions have probably popped up previously and are being promoted somewhere else at this very moment. Find those who are pursuing your dream if you can and when you find them, help them. My finest hours have been when I helped someone else achieve "my" dream. On these occasions, I have joined in the applause and have gratefully accepted the gift of free time to pursue my other dreams.

Don't just "share" ownership. Instead, plot and scheme for ways to give your dream away. Do not just exhort people to participate. Find people-sized things others can do, especially things that they themselves suggest.

∗ *Be flexible—but not foolish.* Be as flexible about implementation as you are uncompromising on the beliefs underlying the vision. Get there any way you can, as long as the way is both legal and ethical. As for ethics, the end does *not* justify the means, especially when the tactics violate the values that form the heart of the dream itself. Consider the CIA as an anti-role-model. Think of how the CIA's methods for "defending" democracy have been credibly accused of betraying freedom.

Question every conventional assumption about implementation. Among other things, avoid tight planning like the plague. Do not let THE PLAN become an end in itself that narrows receptivity to opportunities that present themselves in the ongoing experience. A plan is not a prison; it is a platform for growth. But even in this do not go too far. Adaptability need not make chaos a precondition of creativity. Flexibility is what we want—not pandemonium.

Try not to lock yourself in, in any way. Why should success depend on a single specific location, when other places might do as well or better? Generally, do not make success contingent on other agendas, such as professional positioning, a relationship with another person or organization, financial security, ego gratification, etc.

✱ *Do not be afraid of failure.* Indeed, no endeavor should become too dependent upon "success" in any sense. Most of the winning dreamers I know are not at all afraid to fail. It is not just that they do not let fear of failure intimidate them; it is that they *learn* from failure, and even *capitalize* on it, in ways that transform setback to success. So make plenty of mistakes, but try not to repeat the same ones too often. Always look for creative new mistakes.

✱ *Avoid equating financial well-being with success.* Many suppose that money is the main ingredient of dream achievement. I do not agree. For some, the best way to focus on their dreams is to free themselves from major monetary needs (insofar as this is possible and reasonable). The less money you need to live, the more choices you have in work directions and the fewer people you have to tell you "no." Many see this financial independence as one of the greatest benefits of serving as a "volunteer."[2]

---

[2]More and more people are using the New Road Map Foundation's course work in achieving financial independence to place themselves in this position. For more information, contact: The New Road Map Foundation, P.O. Box 15981, Seattle, Washington 98115, 206-527-0437.

As for funding "from the outside," the less financial help you must enlist, the fewer strings there are to be pulled by outside people and organizations. Weave enough strings from benefactors together and you have a rope, a rope that can choke off the dream. In reality, people will not usually give you big bucks to dream, unless they see ways for your dream to make big bucks for them (or help them *keep* big bucks or in some way meet one of their agendas).

While it may be wise to cultivate a certain modest tolerance of poverty, it is folly to glory in it. Poverty snobs are prone to get uncomfortable for lack of basics. People are rarely effective in the survival mode.

The foregoing may sound quite cynical, but the fact is that life often forces us to choose between making money and making dreams come true.

✱ *Think big and small at the same time.* Do not be tempted to pre-explain failure by setting sights too high. That is nothing more than a cop-out. Thinking small at first is a good way to achieve largely later. Apart from the Grand Canyon, big is hardly ever beautiful or based upon creativity. Large organizations, for example, are typically status-quo-oriented. To a lesser extent, so are medium-sized and smaller organizations. To avoid the pitfalls of size, take small steps. You may need to do a fair amount of work solo and/or your success may depend on a small informal network of people who understand your vision, and who encourage and support it. In any event, if ever you sense that the real purpose of an organization is to preserve the organization, get *out* of the organization—quickly!

✱ *Be tolerant of those who do not share your vision.* You will want to cherish the precious few who share your dream or at least those who seem to understand it. Quell the frustration, loneliness and even anger that would cause you to scorn those who do not share your vision. People who do not share your dream are not necessarily insensitive or stupid. They may actually be *right* and in any case, just like you, they have the right to be wrong. And those who see the dream and do not join you in doing something about it may be neither jealous nor gutless. They may simply be too busy with their own obsessions and obligations. Simply employ the Golden Rule. Offer these individuals the same empathy you hope to receive from others. While differently-obsessed people or organizations rarely cooperate, they can at least commiserate, or tolerate.

* *Avoid taking yourself too seriously.* Pursuing a dream can sometimes lead to periods of poverty, loneliness and frustration. At these low points, resist the temptation to feel sorry for yourself. Instead, pity the poor pathetics who never had a dream or never knew there was one there, waiting for them, somewhere.

Either as martyr or hero (self-declared), do not take yourself too seriously. I dread the day that I am no longer able to see myself as just a little bit ridiculous (not *always* of course).

Try laughing now and then. A suspiciously large number of world-changers had a good sense of humor about themselves and the world, including Abraham Lincoln, Eleanor Roosevelt, Gertrude Stein, Sojourner Truth, Mahatma Gandhi, Albert Einstein, and Golda Meir.

You need not laugh so hard that it hurts. Just be sure than when it hurts too hard, you laugh.

* *Be prepared for some emotional pain and isolation.* Laughter is essential because it is great medicine for pain. Typically, pain is the price of dreams, often accompanied by isolation and frustration. Much of the discomfort will be inflicted by stakeholders in the status quo. Usually they vastly outnumber the "riskers-for-change" and tend to be far more powerful. If these stakeholders see your dream as a threat to their status quo—and it often is—they will do everything possible to block you. In so doing, they can be both fierce and pious (consciously or unconsciously). True pain is the experience of having a good friend assume the role of stakeholder.

Hanging out with optimists will do far more for your psyche than the equivalent time spent with disaster-oriented thinkers (known by the length of time they spend with lawyers, accountants and insurance agents). On the other hand, do not let optimism err on the side of foolishness. We should all consult such experts enough to prudently forestall realistic threats. But in so doing, be certain that prudence does not get out of hand and raise havoc with faith. When this happens, the "cover your tail" game becomes the only game in town and you rarely see a dreamer with a well-covered tail. In a nutshell, if you hear the word "liability" more than twice in ten minutes—RUN!

* *Be different—not deviant.* Keep as sane as you can, but do not overdo it. The primary pursuit of mental health and self-healing is probably not for dreamers. Similarly, "the balanced life" is more for people whose main purpose is to feel good and to be comfortable. As a Dream-Chaser you may have a kind of fierce focus that might alarm your family and friends, at least until they understand how meaningful it makes your life.

Just because creativity is deviant in its own time, do not be deviant just for its own sake, to shock or to gain attention. After all, people will think you are deviant enough without any special effort on your part. Keep in mind that people who smile when they call you "crazy" are excusing you, not affirming you.

The irony is that dreamers may be the most practical people in the world because we often work without much precedent or an established support system. Therefore, we must become experts at discovering relevant resources for ourselves, then engaging them in such a way as to produce desired outcomes. That seems to me a very practical skill and talent.

* *Look backward.* When you get the blues—and dreamers get them like everyone else—do not look forward. Look back. Looking ahead only reminds you of how long the dream is taking to come true, and how many dreams are still out there unrealized. Looking back reminds you how many dreams have actually materialized over the long haul. It is also one of the few things that gets easier to do as you get older.

* *Get comfortable with isolation.* Learn to be at ease with solitude—but not too comfortable since your very first job in the pursuit of your dream will be to find others with whom to share your vision. Still, a certain temporary tolerance of loneliness may be necessary at the outset. Indeed, some see isolation as the hallmark of true dreamers. This is so because, almost by definition, fresh, innovative ideas are ahead of their time, or maybe just sideways to it. So, do not run out and hire a hall for your meetings and do not be depressed at the relative rarity of members, believers, supporters and donors. You may be tempted to seek larger audiences, sometimes at the risk of principle and sometimes at the siren-call of "marketing" (watch how some people use that word). Resist all that and remember that the crowds *might* come later. In the beginning you must be satisfied with the conviction that you do not have to make everyone else believe. Many will never believe and thank goodness for that. Often, majoritarian thinking is the death of dreams.

Press on without waiting for acceptance from society and do not calibrate your visions on the applause meter.

* *Be prepared to move away from present influences—but not too far.* It may be crucial to distance oneself somewhat from present influences in one's life that may be retarding dream focus. This could include removing yourself from fixed patterns or situations in work, from similarly fixed patterns in other behaviors, even from some surrounding people who, well-intentioned though they may be, simply encourage the status quo in you by their expectations.

At the same time, you should cleave even closer to friends and acquaintances who are dream-friendly. Sometimes it seems to me that earning the respect of people you care about is one of the most important things in life. But that respect for what you have been and what you are now may well retard your ability to change and grow, by "fixing you in your present pattern." For this reason, at several times in my life, I have won a certain deference then run away from it as fast as I could to another community and/or another career. I sometimes presume to suggest to dreamers that they be aware of the same kind of possibility in their own lives and their own dreams.

✻ *Find a way to reconcile your dream with your past and the things that have made you what you are.* Although you may seek to move away from elements of your past that push you towards the status quo, keep in mind that you can never free yourself entirely from your history. The truth is that you never should. I believe that all individuals possess a core, a basic identity that continues throughout life, and every dream should reflect and express this somehow.

Though a dream may move you away from some of your past history, what it moves you towards is at least equally important. The dream is never completely defined until you know both. Most frequently, the dreamers I have known are clear about what they want to leave long before they are clear about where they want to go, and this can be a most uncomfortable interim.

✻ *Be passionate.* In seeking your true dream, look into your own history. Think about patterns common to your hobbies, interests, work (especially voluntarily chosen work) and other involvements. If you have had other dreams in your life—almost surely you have—what were they? And finally, who were your heroes? In all of these facets of your life, look especially for that about which you were passionate. Passion is where dreams live. (I've shared some of my dream-pursuing passions in the last chapter of this book.)

In conclusion, there is no formula for achieving dreams. Although it may be a bit "catchy" to talk about "rules" for dreamers, it is probably also a contradiction in terms. Strictly speaking, there are no *rules* for dreamers. All we have is information, expectation, hope and passion. Why should we expect more? And how can we accept less? ◉

Those who dream by day are cognizant of many things which escape those who dream only by night.
Edgar Allan Poe

CHAPTER THREE

Location! Location! Location?

In the real estate business, location is considered an essential component of a successful venture. Nothing could be farther from the truth in a Dream-Catcher's endeavors to help a Dream-Chaser. The actual site of their interaction is irrelevant, so long as the Dream-Catcher creates the correct intellectual and emotional environment in which the Dream-Chaser may focus on his or her pursuits. The Dream-Catcher creates the environment anywhere it is needed, in an office, a home, a conference center or, where possible, in a park or on a mountain. Susan Ellis of Energize, Inc. aptly expressed the concept when she referred to any potential dream-catching spot as a "Brigadoon VOLUNTAS," an environment that surfaces whenever and wherever there is an available space and people who wish to dream.

The next section describes VOLUNTAS in some detail. For readers with connections to retreat sites, small conference centers, or even a vacation home with space for several visitors, the process we evolved in Madrid may lead you to your own ways of creating a dream-catching environment. But for most readers, the purpose of describing VOLUNTAS is more abstract: How do you find a place that will nurture your dreams? What conditions would enable you to focus on your dreams?

This chapter then offers the concept of "think tanks" or "reflection pools." These are methods of group support to Dream-Chasers. They can be done anywhere, anytime. Call your friends and colleagues together, and start.

Peace upon the earth not only among us, but within us,
and between all of creation.
Black Elk

VOLUNTAS
A Dream-Friendly Environment

My experiences at VOLUNTAS: The Center for Creative Community, a retreat residence for Dream-Chasers in Madrid, New Mexico, became the very inspiration for writing this book. VOLUNTAS, with its annual budget of $13,000, provided attendees with a dream-friendly environment; the surrounding conditions and milieu to help individuals conceive and achieve their dreams, without much in the way of financial support.

VOLUNTAS' mission was to stimulate and nurture creative, expansive and practical dreaming about volunteerism, and in so doing to help people and societies use their individual and collective strengths to build a better, more humane world. The beauty of this unusual retreat was that it not only focused upon volunteerism, but was created and maintained by volunteer effort. Over 125 volunteers from eight countries and 26 states, over a period of several years, transformed an old house into a retreat center. From 1990 until 1996, VOLUNTAS provided a "bed and philosophy" and a "dream factory" for temporary residents and daytime attendees who resided or visited for periods from two days to four months. An excerpt from VOLUNTAS' "Statement of Purpose" offers the following:

> *THE CENTER SEEKS TO MAKE VOLUNTEERING MORE ACCESSIBLE TO GREATER NUMBERS OF PEOPLE. To volunteer is to CHOOSE to do something for and in concert with, other human beings. The Center seeks to free people from economic, psychological, social, and other barriers that may prevent them from realizing their full potential as volunteers. Social and economic structures and support systems need to be developed that allow and encourage greater numbers of people to serve their communities, their neighbors, and themselves as volunteers. The Center encourages the development of both traditional and nontraditional forms of volunteerism. We are particularly interested in individuals who are able to accomplish seemingly miraculous feats with no institutional affiliation or support.*

Unlike most retreats, VOLUNTAS de-emphasized structure and activity. There was no "program" for visitors to attend. The center offered its attendees time and space to identify and pursue purposes of service, in an adult Montessori atmosphere. No lectures or seminars filled the hours. VOLUNTAS staff offered conversation only when the visitor was ready to talk. Those who participated were invited to take things at their own pace—to walk when they felt like walking (with company if they so desired), to sleep when they were tired, etc. Attendance at the few regularly-scheduled events was entirely voluntary. These events included a weekly group meditation and a bi-weekly think tank. In addition, VOLUNTAS offered resources, such as the Harriet Naylor Memorial Library on volunteer and community development, as well as peaceful gardens and a greenhouse for private contemplation. Perhaps its greatest resource was the wealth of individuals with whom visitors could network and nurture.

Attendees were invited to achieve one or more of the following goals:

* *Bring a Dream.* Those with a dream of community but without enough money to buy it could seek information, affirmation and personal space to make it real and give it a chance to grow.

* *Find a Dream.* Those who sought direction could utilize the simplicity and tranquility to find their dream.

* *Find Themselves Again.* Those who were questioning their life choices could look peacefully and deeply at their core values and philosophy and examine how close or far their current work related to these.

* *Rededicate a Life.* Those who were foundering could explore more fulfilling ways of investing their lives in service in tune with their own talents and values.

* *Renew.* Those who were spiritually and emotionally spent could relax, recreate, recharge and simply be good to themselves mentally, spiritually and physically.

The center offered its participants an opportunity to concentrate on as well as to live volunteerism. Visitors were encouraged (but never forced) to provide "glad gifts" of labor and love to the house and to the surrounding Madrid community. In keeping with the volunteer focus of the center, visitors paid nothing other than what they chose to contribute in the form of volunteer effort.

VOLUNTAS reached out beyond its New Mexico borders. Between 1985 and 1997, VOLUNTAS and its predecessor non-profit, the Center for Creative Community, sponsored approximately 70 "Challenge Think Tanks" across North America, attended by over 700 people.

The clear majority who came to VOLUNTAS during the six years of its existence enjoyed a positive experience. Their feedback described the retreat as a place of intellectual challenge, clarity of

ideas, listening and inspiration. Individuals who signed VOLUN-
TAS' guest books viewed the place as one "of growth and wonder,"
"where people not only talk but also listen to each other," "of serenity, renewal and inspiration," and for "nurturing the soul, revitaliza-
tion for the spirit."

A minority of guests did not experience complete satisfaction
with their visits. A few found the accommodations too bereft of
many modern conveniences. (VOLUNTAS staff often described the
experience as "somewhere between camping and a Holiday Inn.")
But perhaps these individuals were not at the correct stage of their
lives to feel comfortable in a setting like VOLUNTAS. Too great a
focus on materialistic needs can leave little room for the consideration of dreams.

Others found the lack of structure—a welcome release for most
visitors—somewhat disturbing. These individuals kept seeking
VOLUNTAS' "program," and were somewhat dismayed to learn that
one barely existed. Happily, those who required structure often created their own. This solution worked so long as they resisted the
temptation to pressure other VOLUNTAS visitors to participate.

VOLUNTAS closed its doors in 1996. VOLUNTAS' "death" was
much like the demise of a dandelion. When the facility closed it sent
its seeds flying to and settling in many new places. A major segment
of the Harriet Naylor Memorial Collection on Volunteerism now
resides in the library of Energize, Inc. which in this, and in many
other ways, continues the information-support function of VOLUN-
TAS. Even more importantly, as the publisher of the present book,
Energize has preserved for the future what was learned about dream-
catching at VOLUNTAS.

Then, in 1996, I helped start Stillpoint in Truth or Consequences,
New Mexico. Stillpoint is almost identical to VOLUNTAS in basic
process. It does, however, serve a largely different clientele, of mainly self-helping holistic healers, though, again like VOLUNTAS, there
is a primary emphasis on implementation via volunteering. Two
people who planned to continue VOLUNTAS with a very similar
clientele, briefly did so, but within a few years, major career change
and personal trauma sent them in different directions.

><+>•O•<>•<

We need imaginative inspiration to dream of what could be, and all the
implications of what is now.
Harriet Naylor

Think Tanks and Reflecting Pools

Having and achieving dreams usually involves the courage to
"get out of the box." The dreamer must find a way to assert her or
his creativity amidst the rigid reception of those who believe in the
power of the status quo. Most individuals, regardless of their age,
status or educational background, are afraid to share their dreams,
except perhaps with their most intimate friends and family—and
perhaps not even within this small circle. To disclose these private
ideas, people often need the courage provided by a unique environment, one that allows the dreamer the comfort of being able to reveal
potentially unconventional ideas without the fear of criticism.

How important is this generally dream-friendly environment?
Consider the example of the group of six professional and executive
women who annually met to share their dreams in a lovely retreat
setting. They referred to their think tank as their "safe house"
because, despite each individual member's high occupational status,
not one felt comfortable in sharing these dreams back at the office. If
highly positioned individuals are reluctant to share their ideas and
goals, imagine the emotional obstacles hindering the expression of
individuals of lower professional status.

Think tanks (also known as "reflection pools," "bull sessions,"
and "salons") offer a number of the environmental nutrients for
dream-chasing. The general ambiance of these settings encourage
individuals to unlock each other's dreams. In some cases, a slightly
structured process facilitates the emergence of dreams. Each of these
settings shares attributes that differ markedly from typical work-

shops and problem-solving meetings in that they offer special opportunities for growth and enrichment.

Individually, the special characteristics of think tanks may be found in regular workshops and conferences and may indeed enhance the creativity of the experience to a degree. Working together, however, these elements create a distinctively qualitative difference in dream-chasing. The following offers a description of the characteristics, that where found together, amount to a think tank.

* *The absence of distinct roles and definable relationships.* Teacher-student, chairperson-member or other hierarchical distinctions are blurred. *Everybody* is a resource person and everybody is equally a learner, at one time or another. Seriously.

* *A small and manageable number of attendees.* Participants are few enough in number so that every individual has ample opportunity to participate, not only in sub-groups but, at least periodically, in the group as a whole. Generally, a group of 25-30 people or fewer provides the appropriate size for participation and interaction.

* *An honest appreciation of creativity.* In this environment, creativity is cherished more than "constructive" criticism. Blue-sky thinking supersedes earthbound plodding. Fresh, unconventional ideas are affirmed with hope even when they shock, puzzle or frighten.

* *No push toward consensus.* Reaching agreement is not a goal in this setting. No one urges compromise or the establishment of common ground. At the end of the process, participants may differ as much as they did initially—perhaps even more so. No one takes home a joint communiqué conveying well-compromised group positions. The main yield of the program is greater understanding and respect for viewpoints of others and perhaps for one's own position as well.

* *Time limits are not a restriction.* Participants do not worry about time limits (although there may be some necessary concern about the duration of the think tank in general). Subject areas are not assigned strict time allotments, e.g., "We will talk exactly fifteen minutes about subject X." Subjects, discussions, or exercises are given as much or as little time as needed. Participants watch the clock as little as possible and no one ever uses a stopwatch.

* *An informal atmosphere.* Participants need not wear office attire, sit at desks or tables, or even convene indoors. Attendees can sit on pillows on the floor, meet and converse in the park or in any available environment that lends itself to free and comfortable discussion.

* *No pre-set agenda.* No rigid schedule sets the tone for a think tank. The sponsor or convener does not set the agenda for the participants. At most, the meeting is guided by a general framework or context, within which a virtually unlimited number of subjects may be chosen by participants, e.g., "voluntary action in pursuit of quality of life," or "career changes and enrichment." Within such very broad frameworks, the "agenda" consists of participants' questions, issues and themes. The exact nature of these elements is basically unpredictable beforehand. The closest the framework comes to "procedure" is: 1) early attempts to help people feel comfortable talking about issues and goals they otherwise might "hold in" for fear people would think they're "crazy" (include dreams here); and 2) exercises designed to help people break free from rooted preconceptions in dealing with these issues on dreams. The exercises have names like "Question the Question," "Anchors Aweigh," and "Inside Out and Upside Down."[1] But generally serendipity is the only guaranteed expectation.

---

[1] Two of the creative-thinking exercises are described in the following pages. Others are posted in my Archives on the Web in Section III on "Creative Problem Solving." See: http//www.regis.edu/spsmnm/dovia/ivan.

❋ *The "starting question" rarely becomes the "ending question."* In any segment of a think tank, the process concentrates at least as much on getting a better question as on getting better answers to the old (starting) questions. Therefore, a think tank session can be an excellent preparation for traditional problem-solving in that it teaches participants how to begin with the best possible question(s).

❋ *A flowing and evolving dialogue.* Even for the "good questions" produced by the discussion, the dialogue tends to evolve and transform rather than focus narrowly. A discussion of mandated community service, for example, might somehow "follow its nose" to a theme of political expediency vs. altruism; the latter related to the former, but still somehow "off the topic." Think tanks are always moving "off the subject" in this way. The difference between a well-organized workshop or problem-solving meeting and a think thank/reflection pool is something like the difference between walking on the sidewalk towards a definite destination versus taking off your shoes and walking through a meadow in the spring. The latter is often more renewing, and prone to discovery. But strollers must beware of thorns!

If the environment ignores structure, conventional agendas, and time constraints and, if the discussion encourages informality and creativity, it may well be (or at least on its way to becoming) a think tank. Without question, think tanks are not for everyone. But for some, they can be valuably enriching and curiously productive. Why choose a think tank over a formal workshop or conference? And once engaged in a think tank, how can it be used to cultivate dreams? The following essay, written around 1984 by Nancy Cole, provides a free-flowing, thought provoking answer to these questions.

Why a Think Tank
By Nancy Cole

To shake up the status quo . . .To encourage visions, dreams, possibilities. . .To generate what-if's and why-not's. . .To get in touch with our personal professional philosophies about education, leadership, volunteers. . .To get loose from the fetters . . .To move from "why?" to "why not?" . . .To blow the lid off. . . To stir up. . .To make uncomfortable. . . to challenge the comfortable equilibrium. . .To re-examine attitudes, assumptions, beliefs.

What is a think tank? . . . and what is a think tank not? . . . Do we need to start with a definition . . . or with just some expectations? Maybe assumptions . . . Perhaps a predisposition to openness and the suspension of judgment.

A think tank . . .It is the free association of ideas . . . like a slow brainstorm. Climate and participation are more important than methodology. Controversy—in an exploratory sense—is perhaps a more important element than consensus. It is not so much problem-solving than it is exploration. It is like the difference between decision-making and critical thinking. Creativity rather than caution. Let's blow up the dam and build some bridges.

So don't worry about organizing it—let it happen. Nurture the root system rather than focus on the blossoms. Rearrange information rather than regurgitate facts. Wrestle rather than resolve. Push, pull, prod, poke—*don't* prescribe. Generate—there are no worthless ideas. . . . Ask—there are no dumb questions. Splash some bright colors into the gray areas. Think in terms of a mobile, not a jigsaw puzzle. When a jigsaw puzzle is "done" all the pieces fit and it becomes static. However, a completed mobile has movement, fluidity—it depends on balancing the elements.

Why a think tank rather than a workshop? . . . A think-tank continues, but the workshop, conference, consultation all have built-in stopping places—they end. A think tank should rush and tumble and seek like a river. A think tank is not a quiet pond (or a stagnant pool). If you cannot be a river, throw some pebbles in the pond and consider the ripples. Do not expect—experiment.

Do not be compulsive—be impulsive. Do not line up your ducks in a row—give in to the urge to ruffle their feathers!

A think tank is not necessarily efficient but it is likely to be effective. You do not start at point A and expect to end up at point B. Rather, start with all the letters and invent alphabet soup! Feel free to doodle—this is not a paint by number process. The trap is in trying to make a think tank do what a workshop is supposed to do. A think tank is like the time you would set aside (and guard) to get together for breakfast (or a happy hour) once a month with your associates to talk and to share and to do some blue-sky thinking out loud. It is not the time structured into every other Monday morning for a staff meeting with a pre-determined agenda.

The think tank—an ongoing seminar. A place/time to process information rather than simply choose and prioritize facts to support a decision. Allow for differing behavioral styles and approaches to life. Suspend judgment. Talk about thinking. Work toward understanding rather than knowledge. Challenge and support.

ENJOY!

>+4)×O×(4×

If you have built castles in the air, your work need not be lost; that is where they should be. Now put the foundations under them.
Henry David Thoreau

The Support Circle
A Problem-Solving Network

Nancy Cole's eloquence notwithstanding, there is sometimes a role for at least a little structure in dream-chasing. An example is one group activity that I have evolved over time and used in many ways that I call a "Support Circle." It is a process that allows maximum attention to individual participants while eliciting the synergy of group response. One of the nice things about this activity is its flexibility. It can be activated in several ways:

*   If there is enough time available—and 2¹/₂ to 3 hours are typically needed—the Support Circle can be a stand-alone exercise done all at one time.

*   Early in a several-day think tank or other gathering, Support Circles can be formed and meet for one or two periods of individual focus. Then, throughout the next days, the same participants meet at various intervals to continue the process until each individual in the group has had time at the center of attention.

*   A group of colleagues can form an ongoing Support Circle, following the rules and procedures, in which they meet regularly (for lunch, say) over many months, each time focusing on one or two members. This continues in round-robin fashion for as long as desired.

The instructions for the Support Circle are given below, adapted from the version published in my book, *When Everyone's a Volunteer* (Energize, 1992).

Background and Rules

The Support Circle is designed to concentrate the total problem-solving energies of a group on one person's question/issue/problem or challenge. The image is of a magnifying glass focusing the sun's rays to start a flame . . .

*   PARTICIPANTS are 5 to 8 mature, self-disciplined, caring people. There are three roles, which rotate among all the participants:

    The *Conductor* is the person whose question/issue is being concentrated on.
    The *Facilitator/Referee* monitors time, and observance of process and rules.
    The *Consultants* are all other participants.

✱ The SETTING should be quiet, relaxed, casual, comfortable and, often but not always, rural. The only equipment needed is scissors to cut the phone line. Casual clothes, of course.

✱ TOPICS are the choice of the Conductor within a broad framework set in advance by or specialized for the group, and with the following three provisos:

1. Not too technical, esoteric, or specialized, e.g., not "how to improve my three-dimensional chess game."
2. Ethical. "How to build a bomb in my cellar" is out.
3. At least potentially solvable, including manageable chunks of unmanageably large problems. No intrinsic riddles, please.

In other words, each participant has the opportunity to share the idea, concern, or dream of his/her choice.

✱ Here are the RULES:

1. Absolute confidentiality. This means don't even tell your best friend or most intimate acquaintance "in confidence." One exception: The Conductor may give explicit permission to pursue a carefully defined subject area outside the circle.
2. The conductor must define her or his question/issue as clearly as possible. However, note that the starting question may not be the best or final question.
3. Wherever possible, background on the Conductor and his/her question should be made available beforehand to participant-consultants.
4. Every participant firmly commits to staying in the Circle until each participant's issue or question is fully addressed. The reasons are experiential as well as ethical; Consultants learn as much as Conductors.

✱ TIME FRAME: At least two and one-half to three hours, if everyone is to have their turn. Regularly meeting Support Circles, however, are usually comfortable letting just one or two people "have the floor" each meeting, in which case 45 to 60 minutes will suffice each time.

The Process

Step 1. (Done once only, at the first meeting.) Each participant introduces himself/herself, emphasizing the resources and experiences s/he can bring to bear on problems.

Step 2: Conductor states and restates her/his issue or problem until Consultants agree it is clear, manageable, and explicit about any hidden assumptions—or until the Consultant has had enough with the questioning, already! Try to spend no more than 5 to 10 minutes on this.

Step 3: For up to 30 minutes thereafter, the Conductor owns the group's mind, spirit, and experience. The Facilitator allows no Consultant self-reference unless clearly relevant to the Conductor's issue. The Conductor is not required to respond immediately and should not evaluate input right away. S/he is, however, required to summarize suggestions thus far offered, any time a Consultant asks for this. S/he can also ask questions to clarify suggestions, or can call "overload" at any time during this half hour and take a break to mull the input. Remaining time can be used at some later point.

Step 4. During the last five minutes of the 30-minute cycle (whether used at once or in sections), the Conductor reports back to the Consultants what s/he intends to do with their input, with some explanation on why some suggestions were given more priority than others. Many Conductors choose to thank their Consultants at this point.

Step 5. After a short break, another participant takes his or her turn as Conductor, and Steps 2 to 4 above are repeated.

Final Note

The Support Circle is an intense, powerful, and usually productive process. The chief danger is participants with abnormal needs for attention for themselves or their program. The Facilitator and, if necessary the entire group, *must* deal with this.

When we dream alone it is only a dream.
But when we dream together it is the beginning of reality.
Author unknown, contributed by Arlene Grubbs

Collective Dreaming

Even in a retreat or think tank setting, some individuals will have difficulty revealing those thoughts that they have kept forever to themselves. Others may have become so practiced at squelching such creative, unconventional thoughts that they themselves may be unaware of their own dreams. Dream-Catchers must find a way, using the nurturing retreat or think-tank setting, to give participants the freedom, the license, the excuse to release their private visions. In some cases, a collective dreaming session can let loose the floodgates.

People who have not really dared to dream, may find it easier to do so, at first, in cooperation with others. All the better if the collective vision reflects basic shared values so that each participant's own dream serves to validate and energize the ideas of the others.

An ideal community of the future provides the perfect shared dream experience. The following is a recipe to promote collective dreaming. It moves participants from a totally independent exercise gradually towards full group dynamics.

The process commences with an exercise in which each member works independently of the rest of the group. Each individual is asked to visualize his or her ideal community of the future. At this stage, participants contemplate quietly without any input from fellow attendees.

In the next stage, participants are asked to reveal the single most crucial and/or important feature that they would want to see in their future utopia. Participants take turns and are permitted to describe their element without question or other interruption from the group.

In the third stage, the group begins to work together. Collectively, the group is encouraged to seek clarification, as needed, of any individual's input. As this process evolves, the group begins to integrate the mix of ideas and suggestions. Where needed, members of the group also add ideas to fill the interstices left by the potentially eclectic variety of inputs.

The sequence of individual input and group affirmation and integration may be repeated as many times as seems desirable. Dream-Chasers who use this exercise generally find once or twice sufficient.

Collective dreaming may prove a valuable tool for converting a retreat or think tank "attendee" into a Dream-Chaser. Once the participant learns to feel comfortable expressing personal ideas about a shared vision, he or she may feel ready to focus upon those personal visions. At the point where the dreamer acknowledges and reveals her or his dream, the Dream-Catcher must do what is necessary to keep the dream alive.

A Collective Dreaming Exercise Example: Harmony, Our Town

In February 1993, during a three-day Think Tank, eight participants engaged in the dream-chasing exercise[2] just outlined and named their vision of future community "Harmony." Other potential names included "Careville," "Diverse-City," "Comfort City," and "Our Town." The elements of Harmony were contributed by these eight Dream-Chasers. The following offers the collective contributions of this utopian community, with the realization that this dream is not absolutely clear and structured. It is still as much yearning as completion.

---

[2] The Think Tank was held at the San Damiano Retreat Center, in the Mother House of the Franciscan Sisters, in Aston, Pennsylvania. Participants were: Sherry Buckwalter (Eagleville, PA); Kim Hogue (Lakewood, OH); Sandy Leonard (Greensboro, NC); Lois MacNamara (Media, PA); Cynthia Moses (Broomall, PA); Patricia Raible (Cumberland, MD); Ivan Scheier (Madrid, NM); and Linda Sauerwein (Philadelphia, PA).

In the Ideal Community of Harmony:

* Children are accorded the same dignity, respect and value as afforded adults. Children are recognized as models of what is valued in human beings: intelligence, curiosity, expressiveness (the ability to deal with their emotions immediately), playfulness and trustfulness.

* All needs are met. All people (adults and children) are respected, loved and cherished. Diversity is appreciated. People have free choice to stay or to go (for there cannot be a single ideal community; there must be several).

* Materialism is not the path to power. Instead, power comes from individuality, charisma, respect and concern for others. People work if they wish, as much as they wish. More importance is attached to play and more of it happens as a natural ongoing part of life. There is immense creativity.

* The family is the central unit and monogamy is the norm. The laws of God and nature are followed rather than the laws of man.

* Clean air and water and respect for the environment have been achieved.

* Death is not feared. Life is respected and enjoyed.

In this ideal community, there is great respect for others' opinions and a willingness to change. Instead of the current trend toward "delegation" (abdication?) to specialized service agencies, there is a willingness to take personal responsibility for the well-being of others and for ourselves.

In Harmony, there is no drug or alcohol abuse by children or adults. Consequently, there would be less crime, less child abuse, and better communication between individuals. Families would spend more time together and businesses would function more efficiently. People would have greater trust in one another and be more willing to share skills. There would be lots of love!

Dreaming, so heavily intertwined with creativity, frequently gives rise to art in forms including poetry and prose. Two of the participants in this ideal community exercise offered their creative efforts to this experience:

> *In this place, all is holy*
> *because of who lives here*
> *and why they choose to be here*
> *A spirit of respect*
> *A spirit of peace*
> *rests with me*
> *consoles me*

So too, can any community be, if those who make the union choose to belong.

> *The ideal community is one body*
> *made up from many whose*
> *purpose is to be at peace*
> *through love, respect, and*
> *genuine interest in others.* ⦿

We've removed the ceiling above our dreams.
There are no more impossible dreams.
Jesse Jackson

CHAPTER 4

Anchors and Sails

Collective dreaming? Needing help to dream? Talking to a Dream-Catcher? To many, these are foreign concepts, perhaps even folly. Most individuals never view dreaming as a group activity. It is a very private part of each person's daily existence. To share these dreams, to reveal innermost fancy and creativity is frightening at best, humiliating at worst. But the privacy with which people protect their dreams often dooms these visions to oblivion. People silently carry their dreams until they become distracted by more "sensible" notions, until they encounter others who mire them in practicality, or until they confront obstacles that highlight the flaws in their aspirations. And then the dreams become quiet again, much poorer for the loss of that which buoyed them through the mundane aspects of reality.

Dreams need not die in this manner. It is the role of the Dream-Catcher to steer the dreamer away from psychological obstacles, focus on the positive rather than the negative aspects of the vision, and find creative solutions to seemingly insurmountable problems.

In a sense, the Dream-Catcher becomes a type of navigator, helping the Dream-Chaser maneuver and make the most of fortunate winds and turbulent waters. The journey taken will be full of "anchors" and "sails." The Dream-Catcher must help the dreamer avoid the "anchors" (things that weigh the dreamer down, keeping him or her from moving forward) and make the most of the "sails" (things that catch the wind and help the Dream-Chaser push ahead toward achieving the goal).[1]

>·‹›·O·‹›·‹

Life is a series of collisions with the future.
We are not so much the sum of what we've been, as what we yearn to be.
José Ortega y Gasset

Lifting Anchors

Anchors keep a ship from moving when you want it to stay in one place. But unless you pull up the anchors, they will prevent you from moving ahead when you are ready for your journey. Anchors exist in thinking too. They appear as fixed ideas, assumptions that are taken for granted and never challenged, psychological sacred cows, forbidden perspectives, rooted reference points around which everything else must move. When we do move these anchors, considerable creativity can be unleashed. Results can also be merely absurd—or actually repugnant. But, of course, that is always the chance that creativity takes.

The process of manipulating these anchors is not necessarily easy. Sailors explain that sometimes you must move against the current before you can pull up the anchor. For the dreamer, this may mean moving against current mainstream assumptions in order to pursue a creative vision.

---

[1] The concept of "sails" that facilitate dreaming was developed by Judith Lonergan.

A dreamer must learn how to interpret and manipulate anchors. Not all anchors are bad. Those that are beneficial should not be pulled up, for they keep us safe in the oftimes stormy seas of life, and give meaning to our existence. Good anchors include our basic values and faith. Indeed, a dream that fails to connect with these anchors is essentially invalid and unlikely to endure.

Anchors that should or must be pulled up to enable the pursuit of dreams are those that depend upon deeply grooved, often negative predictions such as:

* *The "Only Way" Anchor*: There is, *of course*, only one way of doing it—there is no other way.

    You are dissatisfied with your local school system and your dream is to find a way to improve it. You encounter an "only way" anchor that tells you that the school system is uniquely responsible for your child's education and that your only options are 1) to complain helplessly or 2) to lobby against a powerful status-quo oriented board for positive changes in the school system. Until you are able to dismiss these "only way" anchors you can never dream of a home-schooling option, perhaps in collaboration with other disenchanted parents or even an alternative school.

* *The "They Can't" Anchor*: These people (the disabled, minorities, women, elders, children, etc.), *of course*, are not capable of doing or being what we're looking for.

    Frustrated with the level of temporary office support you have worked with in the past, you seek to start your own agency to offer a better quality of temporary staff. Until you push aside the powerful unconscious preconception that, *of course*, people over 65 represent only problems and care recipients, you will never recognize the value of seniors as a highly trained, well-educated employment resource.

* *The Escalation Anchor*: If some is good, more is better.

    A very simplistic example of this would be that if eight glasses of water a day are good for you, 16 glasses are "twice as good," and 32 would be just marvelous. (Talk about sailing away!) In essence, this anchor suggests that if a little of something does not work, or doesn't work well, just assume (hazardously) that it's because there isn't enough of it and try some more. As long as you are shackled to "more of the same" as the only option, the harder it will be to see value in trying something different as your dream.

You have saved for years to start your own business, a little corner restaurant featuring the dishes your friends have always admired. You pick what you believe to be the perfect location and wait until a space finally becomes available in that neighborhood. The customers who come also rave but not enough of them patronize your restaurant to keep it afloat. You decide that the money you have already invested was not adequate to make your restaurant upscale enough to bring in the clientele. You take out loans, pouring as much money into the place as you can borrow. You end up throwing good money after bad because the problem was not "glitz" but was instead the inconvenient location of the restaurant.

✱ *The Improvement Anchor:* Taking the status quo and making it better will achieve the goal. In fact, more is not always better and sometimes even better is not better.   Improving that which already exists can lead to new problems.

Traffic studies indicate that new housing developments and new businesses have taxed an older country road beyond the capacity of its two lanes. The county decides to improve the road, expanding it from two lanes to four. Instead of alleviating the traffic problem, the county soon finds that the new road encourages additional building and attracts travelers who had formerly used other, less-improved routes. As a result, the improved road engenders additional traffic and causes more congestion than had been experienced on its two-lane predecessor. Had the county attempted to create ride-sharing incentives, and commuter bus options, it might have solved the problem without encouraging increased traffic problems.

Anchors hide not only in the potential solutions to problems, but in the questions that seek the solutions as well.   Dreamers and

Dream-Catchers need to be on the lookout for anchored inquiries and must make certain that dreams do not respond to the wrong question. For example, a volunteer administrator who assumes that his or her organization will benefit from more volunteers may come seeking a way to enlarge the program. The Dream-Catcher may suggest, upon examining the dream, that the program is not ready to increase in size and that the group might be more effective by changing its techniques rather than increasing its membership.

>-◄>-O-(>-◄

To boldly go where no one has gone before.
Captains Kirk and Picard

Unfurling Sails

Fortunately, to balance the anchors that frustrate and inhibit dreams, there are also sails. Sails push visionaries along on their journeys. Sails and anchors perform in a creative counterpoint, sometimes working together, other times working in spite of each other. Like anchors, sails must be recognized, understood and manipulated, lest they be missed or misused.

Sails consist of the signals, the opportunities, and the incentives that help to push the dreamer closer to his or her goal. Often, sails come quite unexpectedly and because they arrive in the form of a surprise, they can be missed or overlooked. Without sails, the dreamer may drift about without any intended direction.

Drifting is not always undesirable. It fact, it can be interesting, and can enable the dreamer to see and do fascinating things that s/he would not have planned intentionally. These unexpected adventures can lead to greater creativity and even to new dreams. Those that require structure and organization in their lives frequently lack the ability and/or the freedom to drift along to simply see what happens. But even those who enjoy the lack of restrictions allowed by drifting must learn to use and to appreciate potential sails that send them in a specific direction.

Some sails contribute to smooth sailing. A rewarding think tank, retreat or support circle, for example, will offer a dreamer the courage to move forward with her or his goal. At other times sails will pit the dreamer against the wind. A creative inspiration may prompt the Dream-Chaser to defy authority and/or to advocate change. Some sails will even require the dreamer to change course. A dreamer who unexpectedly finds that an idea helps in unintended ways may choose to modify the dream to follow that new direction.

Examples of sails in my life certainly include Social Security payments. While they have not exactly had me laughing all the way to the bank, they have had a large role in enabling a great deal of volunteering on my part over the past dozen years. Two other sails:

* In the early 1990s I was dreaming of a way in which "ordinary" people could be helpful to others in their community without needing a lot of education, training, or association with an agency-based volunteer program. There appeared at the door of VOLUNTAS a woman who was looking for an opportunity to teach just such a technique, called "Reiki," a hands-on method for stress relaxation and other healing almost anyone can learn. This woman has been my mentor ever since, and Reiki was the foundation of my present retreat center, Stillpoint.

* At Stillpoint, our gardening efforts, both beautifying and edible, were languishing due to broken garden tools and insufficient soil additives. At which point there appeared a local project willing to give us what we needed in exchange for teaching gardening to "at risk" teenagers—something we'd been wanting to do anyhow.

Good sailors know how to use sails to their advantage. The same wind that sends them out to sea, carries them home again. Dreamers must use and adapt what they have to make the most of their dreams and their resources.

Sails may help the dreamer arrive at the destination on time and as planned. Alternatively, sails may push the Dream-Chaser to a different place at a different time as the dreams change along the way. And in some way, every dreamer discovers that the trip just taken is only the first part of a longer, more all-encompassing journey. ◉

I don't know who—or what—put the question.
I don't even remember answering.
But at some moment I did answer YES to Someone—
or something—
and from that hour I was certain that existence is meaningful
and that, therefore, my life, in surrender, had a goal.
Dag Hammarskjold

CHAPTER FIVE

Keeping Dreams Alive

Some dreams die because they never lived.   Unlike Dag
Hammarskjold, some people never answer YES when the question is posed.   Other dreams die because of anchors, because the Dream-Chaser does not know how to focus upon the dream or to steer away from rigid, inaccurate preconceptions that try to inhibit innovation. Dreams die because the Dream-Chaser is too afraid to let out the sails, to take the signs and signals that suggest that s/he should forge ahead.

To keep dreams alive, the Dream-Catcher must be prepared to recognize these obstacles and deterrents and must be ready to help the dreamer do what is necessary to maneuver through these hindrances. The dreamer too must learn to recognize the types of attitudes and misconceptions that will try to dissuade him or her from carrying out a goal or aspiration. The following materials discuss several of the most potent and forbidding obstacles to dreams.

Do not be deceived or dismayed by the fact that each segment's title begins with the phrase "Dreams Die Because . . .." Together with the description of each dream-chasing poison comes a prescription for the potential antidote.

➤◄➤◄O◄➤◄

Every [person] is called upon to create their own future.
Gregory Baum

But everybody else seems to want to do it for you.

Dreams Die Because
OTHERS ARE HAPPY TO DO YOUR
DREAMING FOR YOU

In our society, setting goals has become something of an occupation, a specialty that others do for you because they are considered more skilled or powerful. Our parents and teachers see or want to see a special talent in us and push us in that direction. Our employers have a particular need and steer us to fill that role rather than the one we would choose or in which we would thrive.

How often have we heard something like this: "All my life, I've pretty much done what others thought I should do, been what others thought I should be, even wanted what others thought I should want." The speaker, in other words, is directed every way but self-directed. Indeed, can any of us truly and fully escape the expectations of others? Our advertising industry pours billions of dollars each year into persuading us to go in certain directions. Hollywood tells us what love is, numerous solicitations attempt to shape the expression of our compassion, incessant commercials tell us about all the material things we must have to be a real man or woman. Politicians and their highly paid consultants sound bite our political goals. The major institutions of society—education, sports promotion, advocacy groups of all kinds, proselytizing denominations (who do deeply believe in their religions)—exist largely to persuade us to subscribe to their vision.

The pressure is immensely powerful and persuasive. For example, it is estimated that the average person is bombarded with twenty thousand commercials per year, not to mention the "hidden messages" in sitcoms, "news programs," etc. The wonder is that anyone survives such assaults on mind and soul. The miracle is, with so many people happy to dream for you, that anyone has an independent creative thought.

Dream-Catchers should not find it too difficult to spot a person affected with a hand-me-down dream. Frequently, it will also be possible to identify the source of the dream from the media, mainline political institutions, etc.

Upon encountering a pre-masticated goal, the Dream-Catcher should attempt to surface the issue for discussion. At the very least, the Dream-Chaser should be made aware of the fact that the dream is not truly his or her own. Some dreamers may feel comfortable with second-hand dreams. A Dream-Catcher who encounters such an individual should not attempt to help "find a new dream." It is not necessary to presume any less worth in a dream that is the pressured product of society's dream factory. Some of these goals—maybe quite a few of them—are good goals. Thus, it could be very wrong to discourage a retiree from volunteering twenty hours a week simply because s/he was motivated to do so by a powerful national "propaganda" machine's message for retired seniors. Moreover, insofar as a person's goal is a direct reflection of a mainline institutional promotion, there is less chance that s/he will have to undergo the stresses of being seen as "different." There may also be more chances to get significant implementary help as an ally of a mainline institution, than as a renegade or challenger. Conformity with societal expectation is appropriate for some dreamers, and the Dream-Catcher must learn to recognize and to encourage those whose dream-fulfillment would benefit more from affiliation than independence.

However, when the Dream-Catcher—and more importantly the Dream-Chaser—perceives that independence from social pressure is desirable in choosing and activating a dream, the strategy must change. In such cases, the Dream-Catcher should help the dreamer cultivate a conceptual counter-culture, sometimes referred to as an "affirmation cluster": an environment and a social group in which the dreamer is encouraged and supported in thinking more independently.

For these individuals, the Dream-Catcher may help by providing a retreat or think tank, perhaps a "Brigadoon VOLUNTAS" or any type of dream-nurturing environment. For those who already feel comfortable with the ability to dream for themselves, the Dream-Catcher should try to create an atmosphere that helps to inspire and to affirm these people in their own aspirations; to give them clear permission to dream. It is these individuals who will undoubtedly have the more difficult path. They will make their own choices, possibly unpopular ones. To encourage and inspire, Dream-Catchers should refer their dreamers to the words of Antonio Machado: "We make the path by walking." Similar words were offered by Saint Augustine (originally in Latin) when he said: *Solvitur Ambulando,* "It is solved by walking."

In accordance with these words, for some, if not for all, there comes a point at which we must make our *own* path, a point at which we cannot delegate but must dream for ourselves.

>‹‹›‹O‹‹›‹‹

Energy creates energy. It is by spending oneself that one becomes rich.
Sarah Bernhardt

Dreams Die Because of an
INABILITY TO CONCENTRATE

Though fascinating to watch, hummingbirds do not have much lifting power. Sometimes dreams die because the dreamer cannot focus sufficiently, or cannot or will not devote consistent energy to the tasks involved. Such people characteristically "spread themselves too thin," or "have too many irons in the fire." The inability to concentrate is largely a personality trait; that is, it will tend to prevent effective concentration even when in the absence of outside situational distractions.

It is hard to find descriptive terms for these individuals that are not "loaded" with either complimentary or uncomplimentary connotations. For example, words such as "dilettante," "hummingbird," and "scatterbrain," are balanced by "tasting life to the fullest," and "Renaissance woman," etc. As for the last example, being multi-talented is sometimes a large part of the problem, because such a person is often pulled in many directions and is given positive feedback for her diversity. As Dream-Catcher, I would almost rather assist an apparently "untalented" person than a multi-talented individual (although I do not actually believe that a genuinely untalented person exists).

The hummingbird predilection is usually quite easy to spot, via sheer variety of involvement, a somewhat scattered lifestyle, and a characteristic extreme busyness (to distinguish from the typically hectic average in contemporary Western society). For this type of individual, expect to see many dreams, flickering in and out of attention.

The Dream-Catcher should not surrender upon encountering a hummingbird type—at least not before exploring a few avenues including the following:

* Recognize that some people *are* capable of juggling many projects at once, successfully. Take some time to get to know your Dream-Chaser in order to learn whether s/he falls within this category.

* Look for a common pattern running through the apparent diversity, e.g., a hatred of injustice, a love of the outdoors, a fascination with trying to understand people, etc. If you can identify a common theme, you can possibly ignore the superficial differences and can treat all of the projects as a unified goal.

* Seek out projects that have less need of constant, consistent attention.

* Consider pairing the Dream-Chaser with another, more focused dreamer, or with a group that shares the same vision.

* If none of the foregoing alternatives (or those of the Dream-Catcher's own invention) succeed, suggest that the Dream-Chaser attempt to drop some of the activities that are less important to him or her than others. (Good luck with this one. I personally cannot recall having much success with this alternative.)

Finally, Dream-Catchers should recognize that, on occasion, *extreme* busyness can be a symptom of free-floating anxiety. If you feel competent to judge this, and to raise the issue sensitively, you should consider doing so. Depending upon the reaction you receive, you may contemplate recommending that the Dream-Chaser seek professional counseling to help deal with this issue.

>·◄›‹O›‹›·◄

Don't be afraid of the space between your dreams and reality.
If you can dream it, you can make it so.
Belva Davis

Dreams Die Because of
DISTRACTIONS FROM THE ENVIRONMENT

"Give us peace, thy most precious gift." This is the prayer I recall most clearly from all those I heard in religious services. It could quite easily qualify as "the dreamer's prayer"—a plea for some quiet, uninterrupted time for reflection. The prayer need not request total isolation, such as one might find at the top of a mountain. In any event, even mountaintops, including Everest itself (!) have become crowded and littered these days.

The islands of tranquility in our world serve our needs quite well. These include our churches, synagogues, mosques, temples, retreat centers, and gardens. Even truly quiet neighborhoods within towns and cities have become precious bastions from the noise and distractions of everyday existence. Unfortunately, these islands seem to be shrinking relative to civilization as a whole.

Indeed, modern Western Society, certainly including the United States, can plausibly be viewed as a virtual conspiracy against peace. At any time or place, one's concentration can be shattered by traffic noises, sirens, boom boxes, construction sounds, ringing cellular phones, etc. Our favorite haunts become noisy bars or restaurants where it is virtually impossible to have a serious conversation.

The perfect solution to the invading noise and distraction would be the proliferation of a multitude of retreat centers, places accessible to all where individuals could find a spot for quiet reflection. However, this may not come to pass until sometime in the distant future. In the meantime, Dream-Catchers should help their dreamers learn to find peace in the midst of their everyday environments. The following are a few suggestions from which both dreamers and Dream-Catchers can benefit.

* Protect some regular quiet time for yourself, fiercely if necessary.

* Have a quiet place in your own home, with at least temporary refuge for renewal and reflection.

* Find processes that can insulate you against the noises of society, such as meditation, yoga, running, listening to peaceful music, and walking in quiet places.

* Find your level of surrounding serenity. Too much quiet can itself be distracting. Most of us have become quite noise-adapted and cannot bear too much peace. Some individuals are so chaos-adapted that they need interruption and distraction from the outside in order to function cognitively. In these cases, the Dream-Catcher might provide the appropriate music with earphones for the dreamer accompanied by a good set of earplugs for the Dream-Catcher.

Ultimately, a Dream-Chaser's success in finding some quiet time will depend less upon the suggestions offered by the Dream-Catcher and more upon the dreamer's own will to seek peace.

>-<>•O•<>-<

Human kind cannot stand much reality.
T.S. Eliot

Dreams Die Because
THEY ARE ESCAPE FANTASIES

Actually a "vacation from reality" can sometimes be a relief from the stress of life-as-it-is, if the surcease is temporary and understood as essentially illusory. Too much escape into fantasy, however, does not make for success in achieving dreams and can, in fact, verge on the pathological. So, paradoxical as it might seem, dreamers must be realists first of all, even when it hurts or disappoints. The Dream-Catcher should honor all the hope heard in the dream, all the fragile yearning for a vision that might, at first glance, seem well nigh unattainable. But beyond a certain point, s/he must be able to see where healthy imagination becomes mainly escape from unpleasant reality, rather than realistic movement toward a new and better one.

The line between these two states of mind is often subtle. The manner in which a person describes his or her life can assist the Dream-Catcher in making some educated guesses about the Dream-Chaser's attitude. An overactive imagination may be another clue to one who is more interested in escape than in productive change.

To properly assess the Dream-Chaser's frame of mind, the Dream-Catcher should employ some gentle, yet persistent reality testing. An escapist dream, for example, is unlikely to be "thought through" on anything but a superficial level. Characterized by unrealistic goals and methodologies, these dreams lack substance. When confronted with the opportunity to carry out their dream, or even to concretely plan a process, escapist dreamers tend to be vague and evasive.

When escapism predominates a Dream-Chaser's vision, the Dream-Catcher should first try to encourage the dreamer to transform the vision into something related yet more realistic. This can be accomplished by reducing the proportions of the dream, e.g., from saving the world to saving the neighborhood, or some part of it. Unfortunately, this reality transformation frequently fails, especially for the dreamer for whom fantasy is the real goal. In such cases, the Dream-Catcher might resort to shifting gears from serious implementation of the vision to aesthetic appreciation of the fantasy. This should be attempted in as subtle a manner as possible to avoid an obvious display of the shift from dream to daydream.

>·◄)·◄O◄(▶·◄

To dare is to lose one's footing momentarily. Not to dare is to lose oneself.
Soren Kierkegaard

Dreams Die Because of
PERFECTIONISM and FEAR OF FAILURE

"Climb every mountain . . ."—but don't start with Everest! Sometimes, dreams die of rigid perfectionism. Compromise becomes a dirty word. The dreamer must have it all—anything less than complete success equates with failure. Yet, in our imperfect world, insistence on "all or nothing at all" practically *guarantees* nothing at all. Thus, the Dream-Catcher should assist the dreamer in recognizing the merits of partial fulfillment in the spirit of "half a loaf is better than none." Moreover, partial achievement may be a foot in the door, a beachhead, a way-station on the path to the fuller vision.

Fear of failure may be one of the most potent anti-dreaming agents. Often the anticipation of failure is worse than the reality. Failures frequently amount to nothing more than setbacks and sometimes result in new opportunities. Even failures that appear devastating when they first occur, may retrospectively transform into beneficial experiences.

Consider, for example, the young attorney who suffers the humiliation of being fired from her first job out of law school because of inadequacies in her writing abilities. Angry and determined, she commits herself to redeeming her self-esteem and consequently takes every opportunity to improve her writing skills. As time passes, she finds that she devotes more time to writing than to courtroom work, and shifts her focus to the research, writing and editing of legal materials. In the process, she not only improves the quality of her writing, but finds that she prefers writing to law. Still insecure about her writing abilities, she nonetheless finds herself much happier in her new career as a writer and editor. Her first humiliating "failure" ultimately helps her become successful at a profession that makes her far happier than the one she originally pursued.

Thus, creative thinking helps to display the multiple facets of a potential setback. Failure need not be perceived as final when it shows a new aspect of a dream, a new direction, or a new approach.

Dream-Chasers need to expect some failures, to realize that the pursuit of dreams will inevitably result in a mosaic of "surprises," including: 1) things that work out better than expected; 2) things that turn out worse (failures) than expected; and 3) and some that just turn out to be *un*expected, neither of a positive nor negative bent. The simple, open-minded *expectation of "surprises"* (albeit an oxymoron) helps to put failure in perspective.

Inevitably some failures will turn out to be just plain failures and no amount of glossing over, heartening philosophies or anecdotes will mitigate the unpleasantness of these experiences. Some never lead to future successes and lead to no greater wisdom than "I'll never do that again." In some cases, when failures amount to walls across the upward path, the best resort is to try a new path, a different mountain, or perhaps even just stick to the flatlands.

An inability to appreciate partial failure as partial success sometimes may signal counter-productive rigidity or simple ignorance of how reality works. It may also be a somewhat subconscious method of pre-explaining failure. If one sets goals unrealistically high or

inflexibly precise, the later inability to achieve them can be rational-
ized in that they were "impossible in the first place." If you "never
had a chance," you cannot be faulted for failure.

Take, for instance, all the aspiring writers who dream of being
published. Consider the attitudinal differences between those willing to begin with a short article or essay in a local newsletter and
those for whom it *must* be a book, right off the bat. Similarly, com-
pare those who seek independent publishers or who self publish to
those who insist on a large and famous commercial publisher. Those
who want the "whole shot" right away through prestigious commercial publication of a major work are more likely to acquire a fine collection of rejection slips than a set of complimentary reviews.

So much the worse if perfectionist-induced frustration continues
long enough to tempt more and more desperate long-shot short-cuts.
Individuals who fall into this trap are more likely to find themselves
in prison cells than in executive suites.

The Dream-Catcher assists the dreamer by instilling a *way-station
philosophy*, a means of reducing the proportion of the dream and
helping the Dream-Chaser to learn to accept partial accomplishments
as measures of success rather than failure. In other words, while
Superman may leap high buildings in a single bound, the rest of us
usually have to take it one step at time. The following materials offer
a few examples of this philosophy:

* A village needs and deserves a full-service post office. Rather
than holding out for this facility and accepting nothing less, the
community could work for and accept a much more feasible con-
tract postal substation in the local general store. The compromise
would serve the village far more than no facility and frequent use
of the substation is likely to further document the need for full
postal service in the future.

* A young mother dreams of owning her own catering business
outright, but realistically, such an independent enterprise is years
away. She could benefit greatly by taking advantage of an opportunity to open a business with a partner she trusts and believes to

be competent. (Even the way-station principle can involve some risk, realistically taken.)

*   A group of friends wishes to establish a women's spiritual center. Construction of an appropriate building will cost at least $150,000 and raising that amount promises to be a long and difficult process. Instead of abandoning the dream, or doing nothing until the funding becomes available, the group can move farther toward their goal by accepting offers from those interested in providing the use of their homes on a rotating basis.

The foregoing examples suggest three other positive points about way-station thinking.

1. It can provide valuable "test run" feedback on the more complete version of the dream. Thus, being in business with a partner may yield experience—perhaps even the experience that suggests that one should consider focusing on another type of business. The women's spiritual center's sojourning in people's homes may suggest the advantages of a more homelike atmosphere for the future facility.

2. The ongoing effort can help the dream to establish credibility. If the postal sub-station becomes busy enough, it will enhance the justification for a full-service post office. A potential donor who sees living evidence of the accomplishments of the women's spiritual center may be more inclined to donate generously.

3. In a test run, dreamers can "learn the ropes"—and build the capabilities needed for a larger-scale operation. For that matter, the inevitable mistakes that must be made will take place on a smaller scale and are much less likely to be irreversible.

Despite its advantages, the way-station approach can also lead to two potential risks:

1. Smaller-scale dreams and compromises can lead to distractions. For example, the partner in the catering business might not get along well with her business partner, and may mistake the resulting discord as a sign that she is not suited for business.

2. Significant satisfaction with the partial dream may lessen the motivation to achieve the ultimate goal. Thus, the postal sub-station may succeed so well that people lose interest in applying for a full-service post office. In most cases, this may not prove to be so tragic a result. If the view from halfway up the mountain is good enough, save your energy for other mountains.

Accepting the way-station philosophy tends to be one of the most difficult tasks for perfectionist Dream-Chasers. The Dream-Catcher who works with a perfectionist should start out by recognizing that perfectionism can rarely be changed. It is usually a fairly constant, ingrained characteristic. However, perfectionists are frequently quite self-aware, and tend to be able to recognize the trait within themselves. Often, they feel relatively comfortable talking about this characteristic as well as methods for dealing with it.

Upon encountering a perfectionist with a relatively high level of insight, the Dream-Catcher may choose to start by discussing this section of the book, or perhaps even reading this section together with the dreamer. The Dream-Catcher may be pleasantly surprised to find how readily many perfectionists grasp the way-station principle—the theory that less than full achievement of a goal can be understood as progress towards the goal rather than as defeat.

Once the perfectionist understands the way-station philosophy, the Dream-Catcher should ask or work with the dreamer to take the ultimate goal and to break it down into plausible steps. In this exercise, the Dream-Catcher hopes to show the dreamer that the ultimate goal does not happen all at once, and what falls short of the final prize can nevertheless lead eventually to success.

If the perfectionist dreamer deals well with this approach, the Dream-Catcher can try to take the exercise one step further, by asking the dreamer to develop several alternate step-wise paths to his or her goal. This approach can lead to an even more flexible acceptance of a wide variety of events and situations as way-stations.

When working with perfectionists, Dream-Catchers are bound to meet up with varying degrees of success. At some point, almost all Dream-Catchers will throw up their hands in frustration. The typical "hands-up" scenario involves rigidly perfectionist pressure coming not from the dreamer personally but mainly from an outside source, such as a funding entity or a supervisor. In these cases, quitting may be the best advice, although it is often advice that is easier to give than to receive.

>·<>·O·<>·<

Clearly goodness is not necessarily rewarded with acceptance. To concern oneself only with acceptance is not to look into the distance. To learn and unceasingly endeavor, does not that give satisfaction? And if companions come to you from far away, is not that too a ground for rejoicing? And to not grow embittered if people do not applaud you, is not that too noble? I will not grieve that everyone does not know me; I should grieve only if I did not know the others.

Confucius at His Retreat

Dreams Die Because They Are
CRIPPLED BY CRAVING FOR GLORY

We all need a reasonable amount of recognition. The disasters come when the need for praise becomes predominant or even obsessive. When two or more glory hounds try to occupy the same project space, there is likely to be more fighting than functioning. Even when only one glory-hungry individual is involved, there is a danger of too many decisions made on the basis of getting credit, rather than getting results.

To identify the obsessive attention-seekers, Dream-Catchers should look for dreamers who have difficulty working with potential colleagues and helpers. Indeed, the greater the talent/resources a potential participant has to offer, the greater may be the threat to the glory hound! So, credit-oriented Dream-Chasers tend to be "lone arrangers" and solo operators. Colleagues, if any, are token when it comes to serious decision-making. Dream-Catchers should also look out for those whose conversations feature a predominance of "I" and "me." Finally, glory-seekers rarely, if ever, give others more than perfunctory credit for anything of value, unless the other individual happens to be deceased.

Credit-oriented individuals prove a true challenge for the Dream-Catcher. They tend to soak up every bit of information the Dream-Catcher can offer and then still crave more. Not every glory-seeker is beyond the help that a Dream-Catcher can offer. Occasionally, Dream-Catchers will encounter a not-quite-insatiable person who never received the minimum recognition needed to build self-confidence. With the Dream-Catcher's help, these individuals can at least begin to work their way back to more normal needs for appropriate outside affirmation.

When the Dream-Catcher suspects that a dreamer falls into this category, s/he should first try a little affirmation, to see if that satisfies the Dream-Chaser's need. If this technique fails, the Dream-Catcher should recognize that s/he is working with a true glory-seeker. In these cases, about all the Dream-Catcher can do is to suggest a project, or re-orientation of a present project, that may be accomplished essentially as a solo operation with lots of limelight opportunities. In so doing, the Dream-Catcher should try to ensure that the socially redeeming value of the goal outcome outweighs the ethical questionability of catering to the Dream-Chaser's ego requirements. Once the Dream-Catcher recognizes that endless and infinite ego gratification is the real dream, s/he should move on to a new dreamer.

Although excessive ego gratification should not be the dream in itself, personal satisfaction should never be excluded from the dream-chasing process. Every dreamer should have a bit of ego and should derive some personal feeling of self worth from pursuing and attaining her or his goal. A predominantly sacrificial approach to dreaming is highly suspect and may suggest psychological issues that are beyond the Dream-Catcher's ability to help. Just as dreams can die of glory-craving, they can easily wither from excessive saintliness. Neither extreme provides the correct nurturing environment for aspiration or accomplishment.

>-<)-<O-<(>-<

The chief value of money lies in the fact that one lives in a world in which it is overestimated.
H.L. Mencken

Dreams Die Because
PEOPLE ARE ENSLAVED BY DEBT

"Wage slave" is more than an expression in a society where people have bills, bills and more bills to pay. Individuals battle to keep up with credit card charges, car payments, mortgage payments, college loans, insurance premiums—and the list goes on and on. For many people there is little choice but to work at the highest paying job they can get and maybe moonlight at one or two others, just to keep their heads above water. The enslavement intensifies when less and less of the earnings go toward products and services of direct benefit to the laborer and more and more provides interest to enrich the money-lenders. In this sense, many Americans today have become little more than indentured servants.

Such financial slavery is only the visible part of the tragedy. Frequently the highest paying job available is one the individual dislikes, or at least finds tremendously boring. As a result, the potential dreamer loses his or her motivation, not only for the job, but eventually for just about anything positive. The boredom and lack of motivation are compounded by the sheer fatigue brought about by constant moonlighting, long overtime hours or even the regular hours spent in a boring job.

More hours spent on work results in fewer hours spent with family and friends. Dreaming becomes a luxury. If a dream requires even a little money, or a little vacation from earning money, the debt-ridden person is less likely to be able to afford it. The end result is a corrosive sense of bondage that prevents people from thinking seriously about a dream or even from being able sufficiently to focus attention, time and energy on any dream that may come to them.

In essence, the "debt trap" prevents dreamers from "going for it," from taking the leap forward to pursue their dreams. Among other things, debt burdens require a "steady income," seldom possible to pursue, at least in the early stages of a visionary project. In this sense, debt service kills community service.

Alas, America's consumerist economy virtually demands that people stay substantially in debt. Everything seduces the consumer into more, virtually nothing encourages individuals to free themselves of debt (except, maybe for some, the relative ease of bankruptcy). To their great *dis*credit, credit card bills each month are loaded with seductions to "charge more." In recent times, one credit card company was reportedly planning to penalize people who paid off all their charges every month!

Hardly any place is safe from the continuous assault of "buy more" (which usually means charge more) messages. Estimates suggest that the average American is exposed to sixty such messages daily. The New Mexico State Senate recently passed a bill authorizing commercial advertising on school buses!

More often than not, the Dream-Catcher must help the dreamer find a way to place debt and/or the need for material goods in perspective in order to leave adequate room for dreaming. To do so, the Dream-Catcher should start by probing, as tactfully as possible, whether the Dream-Chaser is currently in (deep) debt. If the Dream-Chaser responds affirmatively, the Dream-Catcher should probe further to learn whether the debt is likely to continue or increase chronically, either because of burdens of interest or addiction to consuming. Experience suggests that beyond a prudent, comfortable minimum, an affluent material "standard of living," or the dominating hunger for it, acts as a counteragent to dreams.

Almost invariably, potential Dream-Chasers must first learn to deal solidly with the problem of debt-enslavement before they can move on to a serious pursuit of dreams.[1] Until such freedom is won, most debt-enslaved Dream-Chasers can engage in little more than vicarious visioning.

><><><><><

Lack of money is no obstacle. Lack of an idea is an obstacle.
Ken Hakuta

Dreams Die Because of MONEY

While debt-enslavement may hinder the pursuit of dreams, the truth remains that some amount of money is often needed to chase dreams. Lack of genuinely-needed money is obviously a problem, yet not always an insurmountable one. Unfortunately, many see the absence of funds as virtually the only reason dreams die.

There is, however, a less obvious and less understood way that money can kill a dream. The lack of it is not nearly so fatal as the overemphasis on it being the only way of pursuing the vision. This "only money" or even "mainly money" assumption results in neglect of other potentially more feasible approaches. Energy is unnecessarily diverted and distorted by the obsession with fundraising. One expression of this syndrome involves the needless raising of an organization's standard of living, e.g., through higher salaries, fancier office space, or more "fringe benefits." This often results in a money-raising overemphasis cycle. More and more, the purpose of the organization becomes financial development aimed at preserving the

---

[1]Joe Dominguez and Vicki Robin, *Your Money or Your Life: Transforming Your Relationship with Money and Achieving Financial Independence*, new ed.   New York: Penguin, 1999.

organization. It becomes harder and harder to focus upon the organization's original purpose. A tell-tale sign of this malady exists when an inordinate amount of Board meeting time is devoted to fundraising, budget-stretching and allied matters, taking over the time formerly spent on clients and consumers.

Not all fund-raising efforts are misguided. Sometimes, to bring a dream into reality, you really need more money than you have. Here are two examples:

* A small city needs a light rail system that will cost many millions of dollars before the first fare can be collected. The city treasury lacks adequate funds, a special bond issue has been defeated, and private philanthropists seem unwilling to donate to something for which "their taxes" should pay. Even volunteer effort cannot solve the problem since the sophisticated technology required makes it hard to imagine a group of volunteers collaborating to build the system. More money from somewhere seems to be the only option.

* A rather primitive village still relies upon outhouses and desperately needs a new sewer system. The local doctor plausibly predicts plague unless he soon achieves his vision of sanitizing every outhouse in the village. He has found someone who will do the work for free, but he lacks the money to buy the necessary antiseptic chemicals. The doctor is a rather brash sort and is not a viable fundraiser. The project is not—to put it mildly—glamorous enough to attract other fund-raisers. It is also unlikely that any philanthropist would be willing to fund a new sewer system even in exchange for having the project named for him. Money is urgently needed and finding it will be a true challenge.

Fortunately, the two preceding examples are not the rule. Not every dream requires more money than the dreamer can acquire. In fact too much emphasis on money can toll the death knell for an otherwise attainable dream. Here is an example:

A visitor to VOLUNTAS dreamed of creating a national museum on the history of women. Initially, she focused upon goals within her reach, working with in-kind donations of space, equipment, skills, research and set-up time. She moved within reach of opening her museum on a modest scale, needing only a few thousand dollars of cash to supplement the in-kind gifts. At that point a well-wisher connected her with a professional fundraiser who persuaded her to think in terms of buying everything on a far grander start-up scale than she had ever imagined. Newly-perceived expenses in the hundreds of thousands included generous amounts for the fundraiser's salary. Quite suddenly, she found herself thinking more about daunting amounts of money than about the museum itself. Ultimately, she became "bogged down," and felt overwhelmed and allowed the dream to die, or at least to go into deep hibernation.

As the Dream-Catcher for this individual, I now recognize that I could have done more than I did to head off the deep detour that sidetracked this dream.

Instead of destroying a dream, a lack of funds should bring out the dreamer's finest creative and innovative talents. Through a spirit of ingenuity and a willingness to compromise, the dreamer can find alternatives to compensate for a lack of cold cash. One true example:

A village aspired to have its own community library. The initial budget covered buying a thousand books, magazines and tapes; renting limited space for a year; paying the salary of a part-time librarian; and allocating funds for other miscellany. In total, the library would require somewhere between $30,000 and $40,000 for the first year of operation. The village did not have that much money and had little hope of raising even a tenth of that sum. Instead of abandoning the plan, the village started scrounging to put together what it needed. One year later, the town library came into existence through a total cash outlay of $100, although not quite as originally conceived. The books, equipment, and space had been donated, together with some laid-back volunteer librarian services.

Yes, sometimes money offers the only option for success—but not always. Dreamers and Dream-Catchers need to resist the reflex that makes them decide that money must be the only pathway to the dream. A Dream-Catcher can help his or her Dream-Chasers by offering examples, such as those that appear above, featuring creative-alternatives-in-lieu-of-money. The following credo cannot be repeated too often:

Do not sit down and write a big grant.
And—
Do not sit down and write a small grant either!

Instead of focusing on how to obtain grants, dreamers should prepare two separate budgets: one in which everything can be purchased brand-new; and a second that minimizes all cash expenditures through the substitution of in-kind donations of goods and services. This second budget would be highlighted by every variety of creative trading, borrowing and scrounging.

Again, in the latter minimum-money budget, the dreamer takes advantage of every item that might possibly be donated, borrowed or bullied. Dreamers should learn to think creatively about the types of donations that can be solicited. They can include within this category items or services that might ordinarily be provided in exchange for compensation. For example, the village that put together its own library did receive some help in building their library in that the professional consultant who provided her services as librarian was paid by the State for her time.

The Dream-Catcher should encourage the dreamer to implement a plan and strategy that utilizes the minimum-money budget as much as possible, leaving the maximum-money budget for (reluctant) fallback purposes only. Ironically, the dream that succeeds with a minimal financial commitment can consequently attract more money from potential benefactors. Funders see the economical effort as proof of the dreamer's commitment to the dream. Obviously frugal efforts show an aim to make the most of all available resources and a sign that a contribution will go toward the goal rather than toward fancy facades, high salaries or unnecessary administrative frills.

To enhance the Dream-Chaser's incentive to employ the minimum-money approach, the Dream-Catcher can insert into the dialogue the following kinds of cautionary points about fundraising as a dominant aspect in goal achievement:

* Fundraising can take enormous amounts of time. Many of us have attended non-profit board meetings where three-quarters or more of the time is spent talking about fundraising strategy and financing rather than about clients or visions. For some executive directors, the figure is closer to 100%.

* In the modern world, fundraising typically requires learning a new and demanding technology that in itself rarely has much to do with the organization's basic vision and purpose and therefore diverts time, attention, and personnel away from this goal.

* Related to both of the preceding points is the fact that fundraising can become a distracting obsession, blurring perceptions of the organization's real and basic goals. An organization designed to increase the quality of life for Alzheimer's patients may think, for example, that it will attract more benefactors through a more modern, more attractive presentation. To create this impression, the organization may find most of its efforts aimed at raising sufficient money to improve its appearance, increase its staff, etc. In this, it becomes understood that "progress" means more money for salaries, benefits, office space, etc.

* Fundraising itself takes money and other resources, and this may mean resources diverted from the organization's purpose/vision.

Fundraising sources often tend to give money for what they want done, rather than what the dreamer wants to do. The clear danger becomes compromising the dreamer's vision of what is needed so that it becomes ultimately, "what there is money for."

>+<>+O+<>+<

Dreams are illustrations from the book your soul is writing about you.
Marsha Norman

Dreams Die Because
THEY ARE SUBORDINATED TO OBLIGATIONS
OF CONSCIENCE

Obligations of conscience differ among dreamers. To each the burden arises from the commitments the dreamer has made either to him or herself or to others who look to the dreamer for financial, physical or emotional support. Real and important obligations include:

* Children to raise and educate

* Ailing elders requiring care

* The dreamer's own health when it requires more than ordinary attention (this too is a call of conscience)

* A demanding job

* Completion of one's education

* Energy-absorbing personal crises, e.g., the death of a loved one, a troubled relationship, etc. To be sure, these can generate "drown

in sorrow" energy. But generally, it is better to resolve the crisis, rather than to draw on the wellsprings of desperation.

Obligations of conscience usually become evident to the Dream-Catcher once s/he has helped the dreamer to feel safe and comfortable enough to open up about the situation. Disclosure may be prompted through gentle inquiries such as "what are some of the main responsibilities and commitments in your life now?" The list need not be long to dampen dream-chasing; one or two other priority commitments will usually suffice.

When the dreamer reveals significant burdens and responsibilities, it may become apparent that s/he will not have enough energy, time, or attention left over for the serious pursuit of a dream. In such cases, I never disparage the "competing" obligations of conscience or suggest their abandonment. Ethics aside, people who attempt a dream in spite of heavy burdens of obligation often find their effort crippled by conflict or guilt. Denied obligations do not simply "go away." For example, a dreamer who neglects child rearing responsibilities is often visited by new consequential problems that increasingly demand attention.

A Dream-Catcher who encounters a dreamer with many or weighty obligations of conscience should be wary of the possibility that the Dream-Chaser may be using a dream merely as an escape from personal burdens. See the earlier section on ESCAPE FANTASIES.

Although obligations of conscience should never be ignored, the Dream-Catcher should never suggest that the dreamer "stop dreaming." Instead the Dream-Catcher could pose one of the following options:

* Keep the core of the dream but consider how obligations of conscience could be discharged with less drain of time and energy. This could include exploring, as part of the dream implementation, how the dreamer could get help with her or his obligations of conscience.

* Keep the dream, but loosen the time frame, and concentrate on preliminary groundwork for the dream project. All the better if this achieves significantly satisfying "way-station" sub-goals.

* Reduce the size of the dream to one that better fits the commitment realistically available.

* Explore the possibility of adjusting the dream or getting another equally motivating one that somehow integrates better with the Dream-Chaser's obligations. For example, if caring for an ailing elder is a major commitment of conscience, a compatible dream might involve working towards the establishment of affordable, quality adult day care in the community. Many dreams, in the first place, derive much of their power from strongly felt obligations such as this, e.g., parents deeply concerned about the inadequacy of a public school system have been instrumental in developing an alternative school program.

>-<>-O-<>-<

If a little dreaming is dangerous, the cure for it is not to dream less,
but to dream more, to dream all the time.
Marcel Proust

Dreams Die Because
THEY INVOLVE MORE RISK THAN PEOPLE
ARE WILLING TO TAKE

Dreams, by their very nature, almost necessarily involve some risk of energy, money, prestige and pride. Dreamers are, in effect, risk takers, challenging societal norms, status quo and conventional wisdom. The philosophy of dream-chasing grates against society's obsession with security. People today "manage" risks rather than assume them, and take out insurance against every eventuality in the hopes of avoiding the unpleasant consequences of the choices they make. The ample opportunities we have to take risks vicariously, or simply as spectators, seem more a substitute—even a disincentive— than a stimulus to take risks ourselves "for real."

Risk taking is inevitable for the Dream-Chaser. A Dream-Chaser should be prepared to surrender the security in conformity. Before plunging headlong toward his or her goal, the dreamer should be prepared to face solitude, scorn and disparagement from conventional thinkers, and intermittent failure as s/he learns the way-station philosophy of dreaming. That is not to say that the dreamer should be encouraged to barrel ahead and ignore the potential hazards entailed with the journey toward the vision. Instead, the Dream-Catcher should help the Dream-Chaser to recognize and appreciate the potential risks entailed with this dream and to discern whether s/he can cope with these possible consequences. A true understanding of what may be at stake need not deter the dreamer from the goal. Frequently, risks exposed to the light are much less frightening than those obscured by darkness, ignorance and misconception.

Not all dreamers are prepared to confront the risks suggested by their dreams. Dream-Catchers should be wary of "bull-headed" dreamers, those who have no interest in considering the potential risks and who seek to charge ahead blindfolded. These individuals have no interest in the costs of mistakes (either to themselves or to others) and tend to be unprepared to deal with the consequences. Alternatively, dreamers who are too faint-hearted to deal with the risks revealed through an analysis of their dream should not be pushed beyond their limits. (Although, they may respond to suggestions of how they can modify their dreams to reduce the potential risks.)

Before embarking upon the dream-chase, the dreamer must recognize the risks the journey entails. Not all dreamers are prepared to deal with potential hazards. The individual who seeks simply to ignore the obstacles is no more prepared to handle the consequences of his or her choices than the individual who is too reluctant to place his or her self-esteem, reputation and bank account on the line.

The Dream-Catcher should help the dreamer to recognize and appreciate that which is being placed in jeopardy. To do so, the Dream-Catcher should help the dreamer consider the eventualities and perhaps also seek information about the potential consequences of his or her actions. As with any kind of knowledge, risk-related information can be a two-edged sword. Too much or wrong information can intimidate the dreamer. A healthy analysis of information from reliable sources can prove not only informative, but actually "enlightening" in a way that helps to calm the dreamer's fears.

One way that the Dream-Catcher may help the dreamer explore potential risks is for them to work together to visualize the dream in actuality and then to play out a variety of scenarios which, in effect, assume the worst. Through this exercise, the Dream-Chaser will learn when the vision will place him or herself at risk and when the risk may be to other members of the community (perhaps even to those s/he wishes to serve). For each of the potential hazards, the dreamer should then decide whether s/he has the courage to face what could be.

Hazards that seem bleak when first considered may appear less so when the full range of consequences is analyzed. For example, could the dreamer who envisioned a catering business face a business failure that could lead to bankruptcy? An analysis of the components of bankruptcy could reveal it as an obstacle or alternatively as a means of making a financially fresh start.

Similarly, the dreamer who wished to open a museum on the history of women might envision a situation in which the museum neglects or chooses not to include the works of a particular female scientist. In the worst-case scenario, the family of the excluded scientist might choose to launch a public campaign denouncing the museum. Although the bad publicity could prove detrimental to both the dreamer's and the museum's reputation, it could also provoke interest and bring new visitors to the facility.

Although Dream-Chasers may ultimately learn to feel comfortable assuming risks to their own pride and financial well-being, they should not necessarily be encouraged to endanger the safety of others. Just as Dream-Catchers should discourage unethical or illegal dreams, they should attempt to quash dreams that recklessly put individuals, other than the dreamer, at serious risk.

A vision that potentially places clients at risk need not die because of the risk. Recklessness should be discouraged, but some hazards can be reduced if not eliminated with a little imagination, planning and "management." The very creativity that enables the dreamer to find non-fundraising alternatives to support a dream will enable him or her to find less hazardous alternatives to carry out desired goals.

For example, an individual who wishes to organize a summer camping program for children with mental disabilities should recognize the potential hazards of taking groups of these children out into relative wilderness areas. Even with large numbers of volunteers to help, the dangers of the environment might prove too great a hazard for these young people. However, modifications to the dream could circumvent the obstacles. For example, perhaps the camping experience for children could transform into a family camping experience, so that every young person would be personally supervised by an adult family member familiar with the child's abilities and limits.

In some cases, the risks perceived by others may stand in the way of the Dream-Chaser's vision. The community poised to benefit from the dream may be more interested in the potential hazards than in the likely benefits. In such cases, the Dream-Catcher might need to help the dreamer find ways to assuage the qualms of the public. Frequently, this problem can be solved through collaborators who can help to assume some of the risks involved with the dream. For example, a dreamer who wants to start a mentoring/tutoring program for children with literacy problems may encounter resistance from parents unwilling to allow the adult tutors to spend unsupervised time with their children. The problem might be solved if the local school system collaborated and allowed the program to operate in school classrooms under teacher supervision.

Risks need not destroy a dream. Nonetheless, the dreamer needs to recognize risks, confront them, accept them and, where necessary, minimize them.

>•<)•O<(•<

Wheresoever you go, go with all your heart.
Confucius

Dreams Die Because of
LACK OF INSPIRATION

Often, for the kind of dreams we want to encourage, people who are not self-confident in the first place must face an essentially dream-unfriendly culture. When dreams do come true they are often misperceived as miracles. Contemporary magazines are replete with stories about individuals who overcame tragedy, serious illness, and emotional upheavals to achieve anyway. Though seemingly an encouragement for ordinary folks like us to emulate, these stories convey a paradoxical message: these miracles are really extraordinary and thus must be beyond the reach of ordinary people.

The Dream-Catcher's role is to show the reality in the seemingly miraculous. S/he must take the role models, examples, and words of wisdom that are everywhere and use them to create a vision-friendly mini-culture for the dreamer. Some of the possible techniques include:

✳ *Displaying inspiring words.* Some people respond to illuminating quotations. Examples are sprinkled throughout this book just as they covered the walls at VOLUNTAS. Dreamers should not only be surrounded by such phrases, but they should be asked to contribute their favorites. Some of the more creative dreamers might even pen their own.

✳ *Providing examples and role models.* Role models and real life examples prove that dreams need not rely upon miracles to come true. Wherever possible, Dream-Catchers should offer real-life examples of people who went after a dream and achieved it. Famous types suffice, but ordinary, now-living types like Annie

Jones just down the road make even better role models. The Dream-Catcher can offer a true gift when s/he can help the Dream-Chaser connect with the role model "in person" or at least by telephone, fax or e-mail. These role models or examples offer the most inspiration when:

- the Dream-Chaser's vision resembles the role model's area of interest (though it can be demoralizing if the dreams are identical, and sole proprietorship is at issue);
- the role models are people who belong to a group with whom the Dream-Chaser identifies, affiliates and/or admires in terms of gender, race, ethnic origin, religion, socio-economic status, disability, age, etc.; or
- the role model or example involves a group that is generally considered "disabled" or at least not ordinarily supposed to have dreams and achieve them.

During my six years at VOLUNTAS, I sensed that a number of our visitors seemed quite astonished and perhaps even a little scandalized that, in my 71st year, I was still chasing dreams. For some, perhaps those of the older ones, I believe this led to encouragement, in the sense that "if this old codger can still dream, why can't I?" Otherwise, whether only a slightly raised eyebrow, or an explicit inquiry, the sometimes surprised reaction went like this: How come at your age your're not resting and "retired"? My response usually offered something like the following: "What's to be surprised about? At my age, dreams are more than ever needed for preservation of soul and self-respect. I have more time and fewer obligations. Barring serious health problems, I've little to lose except my sanity—which never did much for me anyhow."

✳ *Offering a dream-nurturing environment.* The Dream-Catcher can help the dreamer to find a place (perhaps like VOLUNTAS) where others, including the Dream-Catcher, can provide encouragement—essentially a mini-culture in which dreaming is not only permitted, but is positively encouraged and *expected* as the norm.

>-<>-O-<>-<

The important thing is to not stop questioning.
Albert Einstein

Dreams Die Because of
IGNORANCE AND A LACK OF VALID,
RELEVANT INFORMATION

To successfully pursue their aspirations, dreamers usually need a great deal of information. To achieve his or her goal, a visionary must be willing to learn about everything related to the pursuit of the dream—legend, fable and folklore; culture, economics, and politics; as well as technology, logistics and administration.

America itself provides the perfect example of the power that learning and information can have in successful dreaming. Years ago, immigrants swarmed to America, speaking different languages, immersed in a wide variety of cultures and religions. They were all dreamers, seeking a life where they could succeed, where they would be free of the oppression they had suffered in their native lands, and where their children could achieve. They knew that to succeed they would need to learn. They pushed their children to study English, to master new trades, to acquire new customs.

Like these new Americans, current-day dreamers have a unique need for information—valid, relevant information. Like their immigrant predecessors, they are venturing into strange new worlds. They need to learn about the clients they will be serving, about others who have similar dreams, about legal and technical restrictions that may require them to alter their methods, and about the administrative practices they will need to make their dreams realities. Every dream, no matter how ethereal, requires investigation. For example:

✱   One dreamer wants to introduce volunteerism American-style to Bulgaria. He will need to learn a lot about Bulgarian history, culture, and the current social and political climate of the country. He should also be humble enough to explore the possibilities that the Bulgarians may already know a great deal about volunteering, but do so in their own cultural style.

* A group of dreamers has a collective vision to join an intentional community where they can live close to their values. They can obtain some of the necessary information from a directory of intentional communities, but such sources often tend to be outdated or wishfully gilded. They will need to check for a clearinghouse and other information that can connect them to people who have actually lived in such communities or those who are current members. Upon locating these residents or former residents, the Dream-Chasers will need to tap into their first-hand knowledge by letter, fax, phone or e-mail. If the responses seem promising, the next step would be a visit to the actual site of the community.

* A retired dancer wants to start a performing arts facility for dance somewhere in the region. She has experience with such facilities elsewhere in the world, but she still needs to learn about any relevant activity or precedent in the region. In addition, she will need to find out what can be donated, what will have to be purchased, and who or what organization might be a likely sponsor or donor.

Happily, information is abundant and is usually available for the asking. It can be packaged and obtained in many formats: in print, on tape, by fax, by phone, through computer access such as the Internet, from interactive video and, of course, in person. For younger readers of this book (and older ones who have forgotten) I feel it necessary to add that there is also something called "mail" (not so affectionately called "snail-mail" by some). You write or type a message on paper, put it in an envelope, stick a small picture in the upper right hand corner of the envelope, then drop it in one of those blue boxes you see on American streets.

The information useful to Dream-Chasers can be divided into three categories: *precedent, connections* and *methods*.

* *Precedent (partial or full).* This information reveals whether the plan or program has been done before, or whether something similar has been attempted. Up to a point, most Dream-Chasers are encouraged by the existence of at least partial precedent for what they intend doing. Even full precedent might be appreciated if it exists in another community, and does not put the dreamer in a position of "just duplicating" something in his or her own community. But for a national or international proposal, encountering something "exactly like you had in mind" can be demoralizing. Because of this, Dream-Chasers are sometimes reluctant to pursue resolutely the search for precedent. The Dream-Catcher who senses this reluctance may even try to do the search him or herself. Upon finding such dream-kinship, the Dream-Catcher might suggest exploring an alliance and can emphasize the ways in which the Dream-Chaser's idea could be made more distinct.

* *Connections.* Dreamers can absorb a great deal from relevant people, where "relevant" is defined as experience with parallel projects and/or door-opening influence for obtaining needed resources. Dream-Catchers should take great care to make certain that the people to whom they refer their dreamers are "for real." To do so, the Dream-Catcher should verify this directly or at least via the experience of those of proven veracity and credibility. The ploy of casual, insufficiently-checked referral is a game some consultants play. It is meant to convey a kind of pseudo-wisdom on the part of the consultant—all these experts—at his or her beck and call—but in fact it is little more than passing the buck.

  Of all the potential ways to access sources, face-to-face conversations are often considered the most valuable, and most capable of producing the highest quality of information. Dream-Catchers should be wary of over-emphasizing their value, however. There are people—potential sources of valuable information—who may also be hostile introverts who become more than flustered by personal encounters. Other people are not purposely introverted or hostile, but simply express themselves most clearly in print.

✶ *Methods.* These consist of tested "how-to-get-there" approaches, applied upon the assumption that the dreamer has clearly ascertained first where s/he wants to go. Examples from earlier in this section would include information on methods for starting a museum, a dance facility, etc. Also, we will often need to know methods for gathering and validating relevant background information, e.g., on Bulgaria or intentional communities.

Regardless of the category within which it falls, not every piece of information possesses equal value. Pseudo or misinformation can actually cause more damage than good. In evaluating the quality of information, the Dream-Chaser must be especially wary of people or organizations with a stake in putting a "spin" on their input—whether positive or negative. Examples of these individuals would include a Bulgarian organization seeking funding from the United States volunteer sector or a person who has been asked to leave an intentional community. To avoid getting a biased view of the relevant information, the dreamer should strive to obtain diversity of perspective and opinion. Single opinions are always hazardous, even "expert" ones—perhaps *especially* "expert" ones.

Even unbiased information can unnecessarily poison a dream. A dreamer who learns of another's attempts in a similar area may be dissuaded from her or his vision, fearing that the dream has already been pursued. Yet another individual may copy the other dreamer's efforts, thinking that it is the only way the dream can be carried out. Thus, information should never become credo; it should bolster the dreamer's plan but should not necessarily sway him or her from the vision.

Information obtained in the wrong order can also be harmful. For example "premature implementation information"—getting to the "how" before the "why"—can sabotage a dream. Consider, for example, the dreamer who wished to teach Bulgarians about American-style volunteering. If she started out by asking only "how" to implement her plan, she would miss some important inquiries that could tell her whether her dream could be successful. She would be wiser to first question whether and to what extent American-style volunteerism would be of use to Bulgarians, and what she could learn from the Bulgarians about their own style of volunteerism.

As another example, consider a small village that needed its own doctor. The village devised a project to attract a naturopath physician to practice on a voluntary donation basis. In addition to providing the patients, village residents provided free room for the physician as long as she offered her naturopath services on a voluntary basis. The physician donated her time and expertise in the hope/expectation that the voluntary donations of patients would cover her financial needs beyond a place to stay. Unfortunately, the physician's expectations were not met. Although those assigned to do the research on such a project tried to collect sufficient and appropriate information for the implementation, they failed to take into account adequately the physician's personal needs as well as expectations. The village should have researched the feasibility of the plan, since they ultimately learned that the naturopath could not survive financially on voluntary donations alone.

The two examples above suggest that a successful dreamer should always start with a needs assessment, before conducting any other type of research. This can be a valid approach in *some* cases, but needs assessments are not automatically worthwhile. For example, in truly innovative projects, the people available to survey will not really have much experience with anything like the proposed plan. In fact, those questioned will likely offer the interviewer pretty random comments or, even worse, answers that they believe the questioner is looking for and, in some cases, responses that they think the interviewer definitely does *not* want to hear. They might also withhold responses that they believe the interviewer would not like. In any of these scenarios, the information obtained will neither be truthful nor useful.

When counseling Dream-Chasers, Dream-Catchers should rec-ommend that the dreamer trust his or her own experience, intuition, mind and heart. Otherwise, the best advice will come from trusted, caring individuals who understand the dream. If more validation seems necessary, and a small-scale pilot test is feasible, the dreamer should consider trying one. A pilot test will require fewer people as information sources than would be essential for a true needs assess-ment. Nonetheless, the feedback obtained will be more solidly based upon real and relevant experience, rather than on speculation about what the project might be.

Needs assessments often rely upon the assumption that a suc-cessful project must apply to or satisfy a huge majority of the poten-tial client population. There is the implication that such a survey must reveal hefty percentages of people who anticipate needing the project. For many dreams this is a tragic fallacy. A battered women's shelter or a horse riding program for disabled children, for example, may serve only a relative few, yet those few can be extremely impor-tant. Moreover, the sum of "fews" is "many." Dreamers should never, never denigrate a dream simply because it does not deal in multitudes or because it is not popular.

In some cases it may be best actually to ignore current needs as a basis for judging whether a project is truly worthwhile. That is because a truly visionary project is often "ahead of need" and so is more likely to cultivate new need rather than react to existing need. Thus, the performing dance facility might not be a high priority with many individuals in the community. Nonetheless, once begun, more and more people may become interested in and later even addicted to dance.

It may be best to ignore or downplay potentially discouraging trends in data. In fact, often what the Dream-Chaser does not know—the lack of information—can be more beneficial than what s/he does know. This can be true when the data is of the kind that apparently "proves" that the dream cannot be done. Dream-Catchers can best serve their dreamers by trying to steer them away from such advice or at least to help the dreamer view such wisdom with liberal skepticism. Consider how many dreams have happened because people did not know any better, were not warned off by supposed "experts," or just did not listen when they were told it could not be done.

The advice offered by this section may seem full of contradictions. Dreamers are told to gather all the information they can obtain, but not to use it all. They are cautioned not to address the "how" before the "why," and also to avoid relying upon "needs assessments." Information gathering is full of such inconsistencies. Consider the two contradictory sayings:

"Knowledge is power."

"What you don't know won't hurt you."

These paradoxes can live side-by-side because information gathering for dream-chasing is an art rather than a science.

Teaching the "art" of dream-chasing often falls to the Dream-Catcher. S/he must help the dreamer to search, not in every direction, but in the directions that will shed positive light on the vision. The Dream-Catcher must point the dreamer toward information and sources that will help achieve the dream and away from data and connections that will sabotage the vision.

The challenge for the Dream-Catcher is to help the Dream-Chaser identify and access relevant knowledge, while at the same time cherishing a selective ignorance of "negative-predictors." In some instances, the Dream-Catcher may best serve her or his dreamers by protecting them *against* information. This is true because we exist in an information age where there is often a glut of data. A selective and summarizing function becomes crucial here, to help the dreamer avoid confusion.

Finally, although the search for relevant data is important, it should not, by itself, take over and replace the dream. So much time may be spent chasing down information, that the dreamer never gets around to doing anything, or may end up becoming too exhausted to try. Dream-Catchers must therefore help dreamers to conduct a healthy search for information that serves simply as a means to an end and not an end in itself.

>·◀·>·O·<·>·◀

Society often forgives the criminal; it never forgives the dreamer.
Oscar Wilde

Well, at least not in the early stages of dreaming . . . .

Dreams Die Because of
MAJORITARIAN THINKING

As indicated in the preceding section, needs assessments can be detrimental to successful dreaming. Dreamers should avoid tailoring their dreams to what the majority wants or thinks they need. The desire to have everyone or almost everyone agree from the start on the value of the vision and the methods proposed to achieve it can sabotage a viable dream. If the dream arises from truly fresh and genuinely creative thinking, many people will not even understand it for a while, much less agree with it. Many people will actually be threatened by the potential for change to the status quo.

Majoritarian thinking is what causes large organizations to act like mausoleums for innovative vision. Within an organization, a dreamer is more likely to need a core consensus (or at least a widespread laissez-faire indifference) before launching a visionary or maverick project. One who waits to launch a creative plan until the majority of the organization supports the idea may wait forever. Just as bad, compromises made to attract adherents risk diluting the original vision. The sad thing about common denominators is that they often are, in fact, so *common*.

The pitfalls of majoritarian thinking are what make it beneficial for the Dream-Chaser to have the ability, at least for a while, to work alone or with a small group of supporters. While the dreamer may suffer the loss of a cheering section, s/he can benefit from escaping an active booing section peopled by those who distrust change.

Dream-chasing often requires a willingness to be lonely, at least early on. Later in the process, the challenge will be to identify the point at which it may be appropriate to move out and to seek wider acceptance and support—moving from "loner" and "maverick" to "popularizer." It may turn out to be best if others, more oriented towards a marketing strategy, take over at this later point (but *not* earlier). Even in earlier "loner" stages, there should be some thought given to ultimate wider acceptance of the dream—if that acceptance is intrinsically a part of the dream.

Acceptance is not always essential. In the VOLUNTAS project, for example, the establishment of the residence did not vitally need the cachet of popular approval. Because it did not require a great deal of money or donors and was unlikely to affect the vast majority of people either way, VOLUNTAS simply needed to avoid being actively offensive to potential adversaries. Indeed, any truly bold vision might need at first the very opposite of a marketing strategy, that is, a camouflage strategy. Was this not the reason that the early Christians met in the catacombs?

A deep commitment to the dream makes it easier for a person to work largely alone for a while, warmed by an inner fire, and able to resist powerful conventional wisdom that suggests that nothing can be worth much unless it is "popular." At the same time, the Dream-Catcher can help to build a small, select support system for the dreamer—an "affirmation cluster."

Such a small, intelligently enthusiastic cheering section can do wonders for morale. There may even be some mileage in the elitism of a small "insider" group, though that can easily be overdone. Retreat settings such as VOLUNTAS are good places to incubate affirmation clusters. The Dream-Catcher can also help the dreamer build such clusters back home, by connecting him or her with compatible dreamers and affirmers there.

When a dreamer seems to be over-valuing popularity to the detriment of autonomy and/or creativity, the Dream-Catcher can try one of a few different techniques:

* Gently, but firmly and persistently, point out that many dreams can succeed without having to persuade a majority. Give exam-

ples, e.g., the proposed new cure for cancer or the new chess club only have to persuade a relatively few "specialist" experts. Even a dream for a new community center—one that will eventually require the participation and enrollment of many—can begin with only a few dedicated adherents. Planning for eventual wider acceptance and support should, where appropriate, be part of the dreamer's agenda. But first, the dreamer should design the dream as s/he believes it needs to be. This design may turn out to be in front of the majority, or simply sidewise to it.

∗ Encourage direct discussion of the perils of majoritarian thinking as described in this essay and in other sections of this book.

∗ Encourage dialogue between the dreamer and think-tank-type groups, usually groups with a track record of never agreeing on anything. Presenting the dream to such groups will almost certainly yield many suggested changes, expansions, adjustments, etc. The dreamer is thus confronted experientially—and powerfully—with the truth that one simply cannot please everyone, and should never try. Instead the dreamer must learn to decide which sub-group s/he may want to please and to concentrate on it. This sub-group may prove quite small, and in the very early stages of the dream it may consist of only a single member—the dreamer alone.

The think tank approach may yield an additional benefit. The dreamer may decide that the better way to convince people of the merits of the vision involves changing/adapting the dream to incorporate the suggestions of think tank participants. This may prove preferable to pushing the original, unchanged ideas harder without acknowledging the creativity of others.

In some ways, dream-achievement is strongly associated with the willingness to be a loner, or at least part of a small minority. At the very origin of any great dream there is one person standing alone. One can say much the same for smaller dreams. And in some cases, the person stays pretty much alone, unheralded all the way to dream achievement and sometimes afterwards as well. Dreamers are often free-lancers, hindered rather than helped by organizations, especially those with complicated administrative bureaucracies that cling to the status quo for survival.

On the other hand, let it be recognized that, at some stages in the pursuit of some dreams, the resources and expertise of an organized group or entity may become valuable or even crucial. Say the same for the stimulation and support of other individuals.

>+<>+O+<>+<

Those who hear not the music think the dancers mad.
Author Unknown

Dreams Die Because of
CONVENTIONAL WISDOM

Much of the general public suffers from too much dependence on conventional wisdom. This rigidity, the failure seriously to entertain alternatives beyond the popularly assumed "correct" approach, prevents many from thinking "outside the box." Examples of conventional wisdom have been mentioned throughout this exploration of why dreams die.

Conventional wisdom is plentiful and will trap a Dream-Chaser unwary of its potential for blockage. Perhaps the most destructive rigidities of all are a kind of ossified history—those that say "we've never (or always) done it this way," or "this has been proven impossible." Other rigidities that a dreamer might encounter include:

* *Every volunteer project must start out by establishing non-profit, tax exempt status.* This kernel of wisdom is waning in popularity as legislative and regulatory barriers add to the difficulties of achieving non-profit status and lessen the benefits of doing so. In response, groups and organizations are exploring and discovering other options to this approach.

✷ *Every venture must maintain its status as an autonomous, independent organization.* There are certainly reasons why this may be true and, in fact, much of this text has been devoted to explaining the need for dreamers to work alone, away from organizational bureaucracy and confinement. Nonetheless, an alternative often worth looking into is the negotiation for a reasonable amount of autonomy within an existing, well-established organization, preferably one that lacks and needs what the new venture can offer. Thus, a national museum on the history of women might conceivably be attached to other women-oriented museums or a women's studies division at a university. The pluses and minuses of that "attachment strategy" are at least worth looking into.

✷ *The relationship between the Dream-Chaser and the potential clients of his or her dream flows in one direction.* Many dreamers fall into the trap of being unable to see how much the people they are trying to help can actually help themselves or even help the dreamer in realizing the vision. The dreamer who wanted to teach Bulgarians about volunteerism American-style had trouble understanding how much the Bulgarians could teach us about helping others. In a similar light, how long did it take nursing homes to recognize that resident councils could make their own valuable contributions?

✷ *The success of a vision is dependent upon the dreamer's choice of location.* Many rigidities are built around choice of setting. For example, for a long time it seemed obvious that a VOLUNTAS-type retreat residence could only work in a non-urban setting. Nonetheless today many of us know of retreat centers in urban settings and Stillpoint operates within the city limits of the city of Truth or Consequences, New Mexico. Another example is the near-automatic assumption that any organization seeking to influence state or federal government should be located in the capital city, even though expenses are likely to be much higher there. Among other things, this fails to take into account recent advances in communication technology.

Having said all of this, let it be readily admitted that conventional wisdom sometimes has its place. Sometimes, a dreamer will need to write a big grant, form a non-profit organization, etc. The automatic rejection of conventional approaches, just because they *are* conventional is an expression of rigidity of the worst kind. Nevertheless, until certain that these are the best or only approaches, the Dream-Catcher should continue to gently remind the dreamer of conceivably feasible alternatives. One of the most useful observations a Dream-Catcher can make is: "Yes, but are there other possibilities?" (Not that this will always be a welcome question by any means.) Moreover, information resources should prominently present alternatives to conventional strategies and methods, along with mainstream ones.

Perhaps the best tool a Dream-Catcher can use to dissuade the dreamer from over-reliance on conventional wisdom is simply to point out some of the most dramatic examples of inaccurate rigidities. For example:

✳ Until Christopher Columbus sailed to America, conventional wisdom insisted that the world was flat.

✳ As of the 1940s, African-Americans had never been allowed to play professional baseball in the "white" major leagues. However, this was no reason to prevent them from doing so in the future. In fact, quite the opposite.

✳ Finally, take all the learned "proofs" demonstrating unequivocally that heavier-than-air objects could not possibly fly—and tell it to the Wright Brothers.

The Dream-Catcher should attempt to prevent dreamers from being deterred by negative predictions. On the other hand, the Dream-Catcher should also try to prevent the Dream-Chaser from over-reacting so that the aim of proving someone wrong replaces the dream itself. Alarm bells should start ringing whenever a dreamer, speaking of his or her goal, mentions something like: "My father always said it couldn't be done." (Or...my mother, older brother, boss, etc. Choose one.) As with every other dream-chasing technique, the avoidance of conventional wisdom should be used as a tool for focusing on the dream by opening up and validating opportunities for creativity and inspiration.

>·◄)·◊◄)·◄

*The secret of happiness
is freedom.
The secret of freedom
is courage.*
Thucydides (460-400 B.C.)

Dreams Die Because of
FAILINGS OF FAITH

Perhaps Thucydides left off without adding the most important component of this wisdom. The words apply even more intensely to dreamers when you add:

*The secret of courage
is faith.*

Dreams do not happen without faith. The type of self confidence necessary for dream-chasing comes from information, affirmation, inspiration, realistic expectation and the many other tools discussed in the preceding pages.

Of course, too much of a good thing is never a good thing. Too much self-confidence poses a heavy challenge for Dream-Catchers and bodes poorly for the dreamer's ability to carry out her or his plan or vision. Arrogant dreamers tend to be obdurate to suggestion, brittle to setback, and perceive others mainly as candidates for co-optation or simply as loyal, obedient followers rather than colleagues and co-leaders. Arrogant dreamers will quickly tell you what they are going to do and how they are going to do it. They will rarely budge significantly from that position.

All too often, an individual with such a large dose of self-confidence will simply stop listening to the Dream-Catcher. In such cases, the Dream-Catcher's only recourse might be to stop talking. Sometimes this total withdrawal captures a somewhat responsive attention, at least for a while.

Although self-confidence at a balanced level is essential to dream-chasing, alone it is not enough. Faith in one's self has to be balanced with faith in a power other than self. Often this suggests a *higher* power, God or the Divine under any other name. Sometimes it involves a power seen as outside though not necessarily divine, e.g., karma or fate. Sometimes the power other than self comes from the realm of ordinary secular life, including family, friends, an organization, government, etc.

Basic spiritual and life values are involved here. Dream-Catchers should refrain from counseling or making suggestions in this personal and often private area. However, dreamers who believe that they may seek help from or even enter into a partnership with an "outside power" are less likely to feel alone and are more confident in the presence of presumable allies. Dream-Catchers may help dreamers become aware of the extent and nature of their reliance upon powers "other than" themselves (recognizing that "other than" can get tricky to define on occasion).

To do so, the Dream-Catcher could try an exercise in which the Dream-Catcher and Dream-Chaser start by discussing the gist of the concept of powers-other-than-self. Next the Dream-Catcher could ask the dreamer to enumerate the powers s/he views as pertinent to him or herself. Finally, the dreamer could analyze the importance of each of these powers in helping to make a dream come true. The exercise would provide extra benefits if the dreamer "discovered" new powers in the process of the analysis. In using this exercise, the Dream-Catcher should modulate the level of structure and detail to match the dreamer's personal style.

Once the dreamer has identified the "powers" upon which s/he relies, the Dream-Catcher can move on to assist the dreamer to find a strategy and balance for using these powers to achieve his or her vision.

Sometimes the Dream-Catcher will identify a dreamer who not only draws upon "outside powers" but is actually motivated by these powers to pursue the dream. An enhanced significance to dream-chasing may be conferred on the project in line with George Bernard Shaw's sense of ". . . being used for a purpose recognized by yourself as a mighty one." This more often occurs when the "outside" power is seen as a higher one.

Combine this with a belief in the religious tenet: "The Lord helps those who help themselves." Together these two philosophies can prove very powerful, allowing dreamers to have faith both in themselves and in a power beyond themselves. In the dreamer's heart and mind, the dreamer and the greater power work as partners to pursue the endeavor. For example, consider the rural congregation determined to build a new and larger church, certain that the Lord is with them in this, but still rolling up their sleeves and going to work on it as hard as they can. Do not bet against them!

Sometimes a deep sense of motivation may take the dreamer one step further, when s/he allows faith to lead to the total abdication of personal responsibility. As with any characteristic, too much is not necessarily a good thing. One might simply "let go" and do nothing (or nothing much) with the faith that a higher power, karma or fate will take care of things in its own way without help. On one hand, this seems unduly optimistic, since the chance of outside powers knocking on doors to find volunteers, or making phone calls to ask for in-kind donations, seems highly unlikely. Nonetheless, as products of Western Civilization, we often err on the side of believing that we can make things happen only by manipulating or attempting to control events. Sometimes just "letting be" can be the perfect formula to allow a dream to come true sooner, clearer and in its purest form.

This entire book, when you consider it, is pretty much based on the assumption that one cannot achieve a vision without doing some things to or with the external world. If your dream is to build a church, you do probably have to raise some money, pour some cement, and lay some bricks. And yet there is another way, which seems to have roots more in Eastern than in Western thought. It has many names, among them "creative visualization" and "affirmation." The essential idea of these approaches is that the visualization accompanied by faith, can by itself *create* the desired reality. This is not, most definitely or at least not yet, a mainstream idea in Western industrial society, hence the skeptic or even scornful reaction many have to phrases such as "wishing will make it so." And yet, there is research indicating that these ideas do have merit, showing that plants prayed over thrive more than plants not prayed over and indicating that sales people who firmly believe that they will make a sale are much more likely to do so.

In the affirmation process, one visualizes the desired reality or dream, then formulates a statement *that the desired effect has in fact already occurred*, then repeats it over and over, meditating on it believingly. In other words, Mary would not just say, "I wish I would get that promotion I want." Instead, she would say, "Mary has gotten the promotion she wanted." Similarly, Peter would not just say, "I'd like to find a meaningful relationship." He would say instead, "Peter has found a meaningful relationship."

Skeptics, of course, would be unable to deal with success achieved through "affirmation." If the promotion or the meaningful relationship does in fact occur, they would conclude that it was attributable to coincidence, that other factors were responsible. Perhaps they would be correct, since scientific proof would be almost impossible to achieve in such cases. But scientific disproof would be similarly elusive. Suffice it to say, there is no harm in trying. At the very least, the process deserves more research before it is dismissed as invalid. And, if it proves to have as much promise as quite a few people think it does, the next edition of this book will be quite a bit shorter!

Much as I hate to ruin a cute ending, I have to add that, in fact, affirmation and the similar process of creative visualization can be quite subtle and somewhat complex. So maybe there could be another relatively long book written about it, even by me, because in my new career as a Traditional Reiki Master, I do teach affirmation (among other things).

>+‹›‹O‹›‹

The future belongs to those who believe in the beauty of their dreams.
Eleanor Roosevelt

Dreams Die Because
THEY ARE NOT THE BEST DREAMS THEY COULD BE

As indicated early on in this book, there really is no such thing as
a "right dream," and the only potentially "wrong dream" is one that
is either illegal or unethical. Dreams that focus on the personal needs
of the individual are just as valid and potentially beneficial as those
that extend to large groups of society. The "best dream," as referred
to in this section of the book, is the dream that most suits the dreamer at the time and place of her or his dream-chasing.

Dreams are dynamic, just like the needs that give rise to these
visions. At first, they may start out as a glimmer, a largely-unde-
fined, spontaneous longing, a blur. In these early stages, few people
recognize their own dreams. They sense a largely unfocused rest-
lessness along with, perhaps, a few illusions. They are pretty sure
that they do not want to stay where they are now, but are unsure
about where they want to go. They might well have had a past history of success in their work, yet they have reached a point where
they feel unfulfilled in their careers. Doors are closing in their pasts,
but not opening in their futures.

People at this stage of their lives are on a dream-search. They
seek help to bring their dream into focus; to watch and/or help it to
evolve into the vision that will fulfill their inner longing. Many of
these people took the time, trouble and expense to come to VOLUN-
TAS, or to one of the VOLUNTAS think tanks/reflection pools.

Rarely did a dreamer come to VOLUNTAS with a fully developed, articulated and "settled down" vision. Indeed, what dreams
ever truly reach this stage? Instead, Dream-Chasers came to VOL-

UNTAS with visions in the very early maturation process, at the "trial balloon" or "first approach" stages of dreaming. These dreams may well have been on the way to a version more closely attuned to the dreamers' identity, more deeply molded to the person, or to the surroundings and circumstances—a process that may be called "dream-shifting."

Unfortunately, Dream-Chasers, like all of us, tend to be impatient and may be unwilling to wait for their dreams to evolve. Often dreamers will believe that they have achieved the final metamorphosis of their dreams long before they actually have. A dreamer who attempts to pursue a premature dream is likely to become disenchanted or discouraged, when the actualization does not fulfill his or her need. To prevent this, the Dream-Catcher should try to help the dreamer achieve the patience to work through the dream-shifting process.

The following are three examples of "trial balloon" or "first approach" dreams that evolved into visions that more closely suited the needs of their dreamers (with names changed to protect the visionary):

* Pauline came to VOLUNTAS with the goal of establishing an independent consulting practice in organizational development, capitalizing on her extensive networks and competencies developed as a career employee of a large non-profit organization. After several months in residence, the purpose/dream shifted significantly towards a religious vocation. Several years later, that is clearly the direction she has taken.

* George's "first approach" dream was to promote affordable alternative housing construction methods, nationally and internationally. But when he left VOLUNTAS, he was tending more towards a "career" as an itinerant enabler, combining his love of travel with his genius for connecting people who could significantly help one another in good causes.

* Melissa was a longtime successful community activist working within a large non-profit, in the same community for over thirty

years. She came to VOLUNTAS feeling that she wanted to do a similar thing, but as an independent consultant in another community, with fresh experiences and challenges. She left with an evolved dream. She decided, all things considered, that the dangers outweighed benefits of starting fresh in a new community. Instead the "dream" became to stay put where she was, but—and this is the "new" part—with more effective outreach to fulfilling, social interaction.

In two other examples, the "dream-shift" did not involve the vision/purpose, but instead a significant change in the methods of implementation:

* Steve wanted to emulate the Peace Pilgrim and to walk solo across the county witnessing peace and love. After a few score footsore miles, walking "in her moccasins," so to speak, he was back in his automobile, furthering the Peace Pilgrim's message by greater use of the significant communication channels to which he already had access—he was something of a media personage in the region.

* Donna wanted to establish a performing dance facility and eventually succeeded in doing so. Originally the method was to raise enough money to build a separate building. What proved more feasible was to integrate the performing dance function with reasonable autonomy within an already existing, highly respected retreat and conference center that wanted to add a dance division. Reasonable autonomy? Aye, there might be the rub, someday, to offset all of the advantages.

Finally, in a few cases, the dream-shift never takes place. The woman with the dream of helping Bulgarians expand their understanding of volunteerism American-style was able to achieve her dream in the form she originally envisioned. She created a foundation-funded consultation and workshop series, on site in Bulgaria. In doing so, she chose not to listen to the counsel offered by her Dream-

Catcher. (This is, in fact, a principle occupational hazard in the Dream-Catcher role.)

In most cases, the original vision varies greatly from the final, best dream. The reasons behind this vary depending upon the situation of the dreamer. Sometimes, what accounts for the appearance of a first approach dream is that it is a more natural, closer-in extension of what the person is doing now, or has done recently. (Pauline's case above offers a clear instance of this scenario.) The apparently more "radical" departures become easier to consider seriously as the person becomes more comfortable with definite breaks with the past.

Popularity of purpose may be another factor that can shape first approach dreams. The causes or philosophies of groups or individuals admired by the Dream-Chaser can have a significant impact on the shape of the dream. Thus, joining an intentional community is an "in" thing for certain kinds of "new age" people. The dreamer might also shape a "trial balloon" or first dream out of admiration for the lives and purposes of other individuals, whether these be popular or not, in any conventional sense.

Sometimes, the first-proposed dream may be more or less a "cover" for an essentially unrelated personal issue. One example features a young man, with a history of aggressive business entrepreneurship, who arrived at VOLUNTAS with the stated purpose of devoting his life to humanitarian service overseas. His repeated refusals to take advantage of seemingly plausible opportunities to do so suggested other motives. Ultimately, the Dream-Catcher came to suspect strongly that his "dream" was actually nothing more than a disguised attempt to end a relationship. Cynical as it may seem, often the need to do *something* new is significantly related to the need to find *someone* new or lose someone not so new. This and other underlying personal issues do not necessarily mean that the vision is "false;" it may only help to know that the trigger is not intrinsically related to the vision itself.

Dream-Catchers should always be vigilant for the dreamer who repeatedly finds reasons not to take advantage of available means of implementing his or her dream. Implausibly frequent rejections of plausible implementations should alert the Dream-Catcher to the possibility of a cover dream. At which point, the Dream-Catcher should attempt gentle queries such as: "We don't seem to be finding acceptable ways to move your project ahead. Why do you suppose that is?"

In most cases, the Dream-Catcher should avoid confronting the dreamer with the inconsistency between his or her actions and the purported goal. Generally, raw confrontation produces less success than helping the dreamer to reach his or her own insights. As with most worthwhile ventures, dream-shifting of this nature does not happen overnight. For this reason, the instruction: "Don't Just Do Something; Sit There" should be supplemented with: "And Get a Pillow. It Might Take Awhile."

A fourth source of prematurity in dreams is the failure to think through and foresee all the consequences of achieving the dream, particularly the negative ones. The pluses tend to predominate at first. On reflection, Melissa's enthusiasm about making new friends in a new town was dampened by the realization of the difficulties of doing so for a somewhat introverted person like herself.

Sometimes, when reflection itself is not enough to achieve a "balance in consequences," an actual pilot test may be necessary. Steve's vision of following in the footsteps of the Peace Pilgrim was soon superseded by blisters and aching joints once he tried it. In a sense, it was fortunate this happened only a relatively few miles down the road, rather than at the other end of the continent. The Dream-Catcher can help the dreamer design pilot tests from which s/he can, if necessary, extricate him or herself more or less easily. The dreamer who believes that s/he has found the perfect intentional community should still not sign on for a year without a no-strings-attached tryout visit for a few days or weeks.

So, Dream-Catcher, honor the early glow in the vision, but do not immediately accept it as final. Encourage leisure for consequential thinking against the danger of premature closure. The Dream-Catcher should ask the Dream-Chaser to work his or her way through the dream, and to consider everything that might happen in a situation in which this dream was achieved. As the Dream-Chaser moves through this analysis, the Dream-Catcher should watch for flinch points. By analyzing these potential problems, Dream-Catcher and dreamer can together decide whether any dream-shifting might be required.

The stricture against premature closure certainly applies to the Dream-Catcher as well. Avoid the "Eureka, you've got it!" reflex. Although expressions of encouragement might be valuable in supporting the often fragile emergence of the dream and to buttress the dreamer's self-confidence, nonetheless, at least in the early stages, the Dream-Catcher would do well to bite his or her tongue. In this way, the Dream-Catcher can try to create and maintain permissive conditions conducive to dream-shifting. These conditions can allow the deeper underlying currents to do their work of confirming or transforming the early versions of the dream into a more "real" or appropriate one for the individual Dream-Chaser. Again, this is a steeping, mellowing, incubating kind of process, not largely under conscious control, at least not at first.

Dreams come true; without that possibility,
nature would not incite us to have them.
John Updike

WHY DREAMS LIVE

With all the elements of society pushing children to "go wrong" while growing up, you start wondering why so many of them eventually go right. Just so, having read by far the longest section in this book on why dreams *die*, the reader could be pardoned for wondering how they ever live.

In one sense, the answer is straightforward. Dreams survive because Dream-Chasers and Dream-Catchers take the steps necessary to avoid the pitfalls enumerated in the preceding pages. The Dream-Chaser receives realistic affirmation rather than comprehensively harsh critique; helpful accessible information rather than misinformation or none; favorable conditions for focus, rather than noi-some distraction, etc. Dreams live and thrive, because the conditions under which they die are absent or, if present, they are moderated or corrected.

Perhaps the most powerful reason that dreams live is that having them is a large part of what it means to be human. It is not quite as if there were a gene for dreaming. Nonetheless, there is a powerful predisposition in many people to view their world as in need of dreams. Perhaps those predisposed to dreaming see the world as imperfect. Eyes and ears and all our feelings tell us this, even when the mind may demur.

True dreamers recognize that the world is not perfectly predetermined, completely foredoomed to be as it is. Instead they recognize the choice to try—or not to try—to do something about the imperfections we all perceive. (Even a strict determinist must sometimes act as if what s/he does makes a difference.)

For each of us, there is some precedent and probability that an attempt to deflect the world (including one's own personal world) in a desired direction, can succeed. No matter how frustrating our lives have been, how beset with disappointment and failure, many of us can remember somewhere, sometime, something like a success. And so, we can believe it might happen again if we try.

Once again, this may be as much a primal reflex as a conscious philosophy: a gut feeling that the world is not as good as it might be and that one can do something about it, however small.

Finally, dreams live because frequently there are others who dream the same dream or a similar one and connecting with them can prove mutually strengthening. This connection function is a major part of the Dream-Catcher's mission. The good news is that the best ideas rarely pop up in only one place. Rather, when the world is ready for them, they appear in several places at once, much like healing waters push up through springs in many places.

The need to dream is powerful, no matter how rich or poor you are, no matter how fortunate or unfortunate. In this sense, when dreams die, so does the person. And ultimately, the society. ◉

Do not go where the path may lead;
go instead where there is no path and leave a trail.
Ralph Waldo Emerson

CHAPTER INFINITY

The End as a Beginning

Trying to finish a book is something like taking a car trip; twenty miles down the road you start remembering all the things you forgot. Actually, it happened this time even before I got out of the driveway—in this "last" chapter. So, here are some of the things that could have been in this book, but weren't because I thought there was already enough here for you to consider and selectively apply. However, in the commentary I earnestly hope to get from you on this book, please add consideration of the four additional questions below:

* What are some of the things that can happen once you have achieved your dream? How do you keep the zest fresh? Or, for some people, the so-called "creator" types, do you just set them free and let the "maintainers" take over? How does that setting-free process work, anyhow? Ditto for the process of transition from creation to maintenance.

✱ My glimmer is that dreams do build on one another; for example, Stillpoint growing out of the experiences at VOLUNTAS. Another example, described in more detail in a moment, is how Stillpoint has birthed at least one other dream in its host community. Generally, I'd like to know more about that potentially endless process in which one dream can lead to another...and another...and....

✱ This book has been predominantly about *individuals* as dreamers and Dream-Catchers. The role of organizations (while sometimes acknowledged as in the case of VOLUNTAS) has generally been treated gingerly. The next book or edition should concentrate far more on when and how organizations can incubate or actively support creative dreams. At least, we need to understand more about how to stop organizations from suppressing dreams!

✱ I think we need to learn more about the motivational basis of dreaming. Where does the passion come from? How does it impact the kinds of dreams we have and our chances of achieving them? In the text immediately following, "the emotional driving principle" of dreaming is the subject of preliminary "research" on a sample of one: me.

Many of my insights about dreaming, such as they were, evolved haltingly over decades, and I was more than fifty years old before the results became reasonably clear. The emotional driving principle behind many of my dreams, especially the ones later in my life, translates into something like this. I am profoundly disturbed by classifications, perceptions, attitudes, regulations, and rules that block human beings from realizing their fullest potential. In other words, bigotry, prejudice, on whatever basis—ethnic, racial, religious, gender-oriented, age-related, or on any other basis—DRIVES ME UP THE WALL AND THEN DOWN THE STREET TO START DOING SOMETHING ABOUT IT!!!

This emotional button is the raw material of my dreams. Over the years, I have slowly identified the following highly-charged situations, patterns, and involvements in my life that provided the dynamic for this drive.

* Growing up Jewish in a small town in the 1930's and 40's. We knew what was happening to Jews in Germany, just because they belonged to the category "Jewish."

* Among the some six million victims were some of our collateral relatives.

* In contrast, in the town in which I grew up, Plattsburgh, New York, Jews were clearly being given the opportunity to grow and contribute to the community primarily on the basis of what they had to offer as individuals. My grandfather was elected President of the Board of Education; my sister was one of the most popular young women in high school, a class officer and, as I recall, did very well in at least one local beauty contest; my father was organizing the town band. Not incidentally, and to my mind equally important, when Jews were criticized, they were criticized as individuals, not as Jews, as far as I could tell.

* In the World War II military for the first time ever I encountered virulent anti-Semitism, was called "kike" and was only tepidly defended by my "buddies."

* In the 1950's I was active with the NAACP in a southern part of the North. This provided a truly horrifying view of African-Americans being denied their potential and their fullest humanity, simply because of their race.

* In the 1960's, I worked as Court Psychologist (volunteer) in a juvenile probation department. What disturbed me most here was that, rhetoric aside, virtually everyone had given up on these young people even though they were rarely more than 13-16 years of age. Teachers, parents, employers, sometimes even probation officers—most of them had given up on these kids. The

children were classified as "hopeless" and were not really given much support in developing into anything else. The assumption was that they would never amount to much and, of course, this encouraged the kids to validate the assumption.

* From the mid-1960's to the present, my passion has been the practice and encouragement of volunteering. One of the main advantages of volunteerism is the removal of one major barrier to people being allowed to show their potential. Volunteering wipes out the phrase: "Sorry, we don't have the money to pay you."

* Between 1990 and 1996, at the VOLUNTAS Residence in Madrid, New Mexico, my role as Dream-Catcher evolved. Its purpose: to help people reach their fuller potential by achieving their dreams, indeed, just by *having* them without being seen as silly or peculiar.

* Stillpoint began in late 1996, essentially as an outgrowth of VOL-UNTAS. Both have been dreams come true for me. Both are retreat centers designed to provide people with quiet space to reflect on their lives and goals. Both were designed to free people up for further release of their potential to help themselves and/or other people. Among the learnings carried over from the VOLUNTAS to the Stillpoint dream was how best to create and maintain a meaningful retreat center, and how to choose a surrounding community in which such a center can best function.

At VOLUNTAS the goals tended to concentrate on projects "out there" in the community, while at Stillpoint the focus is more on goals related to holistic healing, specifically to make such healing more widely available to people on a low- or no-cost basis. Among other things, I believe that pain should not be the price of poverty.

Along with passionate circumstances, involvements and situations, the heroic figures in my life contributed to the motivations behind my dreams. My list includes Eleanor Roosevelt, Mahatma

Gandhi, Martin Luther King, Roy Wilkins, Sojourner Truth, Miles Horton and others such as Karen Cattell and Sam Gottlob whose fame is mainly in my heart. The list is a further confirmation of the driving force I see behind many of my dreams.

My dreams did not always focus on helping others. In my early life, my goals were largely personal and achievement oriented, that is, to be an outstanding student, athlete, charmer, competitor, etc., etc. I would like to think that the shift in later life towards removing barriers to human fulfillment was a sign of maturity.

There you have it. No dream of mine today—including writing and publishing this book—is uninfluenced by this human potential driving principle. So, I have just given you my button. Hopefully, you are too far away to push it often.

I am by no means finished with my dreaming. A major current one is a spin-off of Stillpoint (which was itself a dream). For many years, I have been looking for something positive volunteers could do on their own, freelance, in a community, without belonging to a volunteer program in an agency or other organization. In its four years of existence, Stillpoint has trained well over 100 local people in techniques of meditation and hands-on stress relaxation.[1] These are easily learned and passed on by these people to friends and families, without charge. One hundred may not seem an impressive number until you realize it is growing and even now is about 1% of all the 10,000 residents in the county where Stillpoint is located. A saturation effect is entirely possible.

Of course, I do have one dream that is a bit more self-serving than many of my others. It involves lying on the beach in Hawaii and doing absolutely nothing . . . . Don't hold your breath.

Whatever it is, may you find your dream. ⓞ

---

[1] The main stress relaxation technique taught is Reiki, with an estimated two million practitioners in the world. Many books, some research, and much Internet material are available for further reading.

Other Books by Ivan H. Scheier

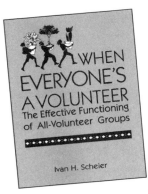

When Everyone's a Volunteer:
The Effective Functioning of
All-Volunteer Groups

Are you part of an organization that wants
to increase membership, minimize burnout and
accomplish bigger goals? *When Everyone's a*
Volunteer shares innovative ideas for any
all-volunteer effort, whether a service club,
community group, or religious congregation.
Scheier challenges conventional wisdom about
boards, fund raising, and membership development when applied to
grassroots volunteer efforts. Includes a collection of easy-to-conduct
group interaction exercises.
ISBN 0-940576-12-0

Building Staff/Volunteer Relations

Scheier helps employees and volunteers in any
type of setting to work together successfully. With
clarity and humor, he first explores the reasons for
conflict between paid and unpaid staff. Then
he tackles the all-too-common stresses of this
relationship with a step-by-step process for
analyzing tasks and work preferences for both.
Offers a great number of creative and
practical solutions.
ISBN 0-940576-14-7

To order these and a wide range of other titles about community service, volunteer
program management, neighborhood building and civil society, contact Energize,
Inc. at 1-800-395-9800 or visit the online bookstore on our Web site:
www.energizeinc.com

Ivan is also on the editorial team of *e-Volunteerism: The Electronic Journal of*
the Volunteer Community: **www.e-volunteerism.com**